A TIME TO LOVE?

A
TIME TO
LOVE?

LIAM Ó MURCHÚ

GILL AND MACMILLAN

Published in Ireland by
Gill and Macmillan Ltd
Goldenbridge
Dublin 8
with associated companies in
Auckland, Dallas, Delhi, Hong Kong,
Johannesburg, Lagos, London, Manzini,
Melbourne, Nairobi, New York, Singapore,
Tokyo, Washington
© Liam Ó Murchú, 1986
7171 1487 2
Print origination by Wellset, Dublin
Printed in Great Britain by
Richard Clay (The Chaucer Press) Ltd,
Bungay, Suffolk

CONTENTS

For everything there is a season, and
a time for every matter under heaven:

a time to be born, and a time to die...
a time to kill, and a time to heal...
a time to weep, and a time to laugh...
a time to mourn, and a time to dance...
a time to seek, and a time to lose...
a time to rend, and a time to sew...
a time to love, and a time to hate...

Ecclesiastes 3

PROLOGUE

THIS vagrant tale starts with a child born to a world of want and ends with him seeming to have made his way. Neither is the whole truth: the waif of early years — slums and common destitution notwithstanding — had just as firm a grip on life as the man of later years; but neither then nor now was either master of his fate — which in the circumstances, as you shall read, may have been just as well, since when he was, no-one was better at making a mess of things.

It is a point of pride to say one came from nothing; it is also a point on a graph to judge one's progress up or down — in my case there can be no doubting the direction. The kindly man who later on in this book introduces me to his triad of nullities — 'I am nothing, I have nothing, I can do nothing' — should have had no difficulty in teaching me: I was something and rejected it; I had something and made nothing of it; I could do something but took an awfully long time to do it. Hence I must be persuaded that at times this exasperating life must have given its maker quite serious tasks of recasting; but also that I must have been loved somewhere, because nothing but that could have got the pieces together in the end.

My father was a soldier, and served for a time in Crete where, as I write, I happen to be this very day. On such a day of burning heat did Private Kennedy Murphy, all of twenty and with his life before him, sail in between the piers of Heraklion harbour eighty years ago. What would he and his flax-mill girl back home have thought of the lives they made and what became of them, as I tell it in these pages? He had fled the slums of a southern Irish city, seeking a life of hope and glory. Did he ever find it? What is more to the point, did he find it after the dreamed-of coming back? I was very close to that young man today, closer than I ever was when he was alive; it took eighty

1

years, a lot of living and some dying to get that close. For my part, I was glad in that moment of proximity to confirm to him, and to the undying spirit of all the people who went before us, that they were right to hope against all hope and right to love against the death of love; and, above all, right to insist that the drudge of their small lives should not forever come to nothing.

There must be stories like this all over the world — everywhere that small peoples have emerged into an era of freedom and begun to taste its fruits. Such stories must exist in the black ghettos of Harlem; in the shanty towns beside the cattle-kraals of Paul Kruger's Transvaal, which that Private Kennedy Murphy knew so well; in the fetid and suppurating slums of Mexico and Italy and India, to say nothing of more familiar slums nearer home; amongst the Maori and Aborigine peoples of New Zealand and Australia, now at last coming into their own — everywhere that mothers and fathers, brothers and sisters, sons and lovers try to make a life of hope out of a life of nothing, a life of glory out of nothing but dreams. Only a few will. They must pray to God against the odds, as the people of our race prayed when there was nothing for them but death and starvation and nettles by the roadside, or at best the coffin-ships across 'that bowl of bitter tears' at the end of all their praying.

You may wonder at what may seem the disproportionate role given to language in the lives of small peoples, as I give it in this book. That is part of the tale I have to tell; and, while not being a bore or a bellyacher about it, it is a part one must tell with love. 'My wild Irish rose, the sweetest flower that grows' is neither wild nor beautiful without that. Other peoples can fill in their own tales: I hope they do so with as much heart as did the Scots peot Hugh MacDiarmid, who could turn his mind from the great flowers of all the world and choose 'the little white rose of Scotland that smells sweetly and breaks the heart'.

Of the two me's in these pages — the waif of the early years who was lucky to survive in an unequal world, and the man of later times — it is hard to tell which is truer to the real me, the one I really am. At what point does one stop the clock and say, 'that's the whole person, the one which has past, present and future all wrapped into one'? At any point along the way, I might have stopped it that way — and been wrong. None of us knows what the future holds, and a week is a long time in more than politics. There is always tomorrow, always new vistas and new horizons beyond the rising hill. Me, I have seen so many I never thought were there that it may not be foolish to hope that there are still some more to come. So it is best to stay around and be ready for the hope that springs eternal.

There is a time of year that I look forward to above all others. It's a bleak time, with the ice still in the air, but the New Year is past and then, on the way home one evening, you see a snow-drop in a garden, pushing its head above the ground; and when you look up, there it is: a little light in the sky. That is what this book is about.

We are lucky, those of us who live to hear the 'still, sad music of humanity', if we have the wit to know that that is what we are hearing. I had no-one to teach me such things — does anyone ever? And when I go about the house now, spouting Shakespeare and Keats and Aogán Ó Rathaile and the blind Milton, and singing songs about the dead I loved though I never knew them, and the living I love though they will never know, I wonder to God what sort of a crazy lot I came out of at all, at all, with nothing but the madness of such things upon my mind. Yet I am glad. It was a wild mixture, but the patient lived — and through it all will say it was worth it, and he was happy.

PART ONE

1

CHILD OF MISCHANCE

ONE HEARS of people dying, or seeming to die, then coming back for a brief recovery to die really the second time. I have yet to meet anyone who did what I did: be born twice. The first of these was many years before I arrived — the boy, I am told, the image of me and certainly with my name. But those were the years of the black epidemics that wiped out whole families, and that William Murphy — for so I was christened, though I now use the Irish form — was wiped out along with thousands of others in one such deadly foray. Mother never spoke about him at all as she did about some of her other children who died in like circumstances in infancy; neither did Father, which is a little more surprising since with that name he should have been the apple of his eye: for it so happens that that was also his own father's name, a man to whom he was so deeply attached that in later years he could never speak about him without weeping.

That William Murphy, my grandfather, was, we were told, the smartest man in Cork. 'That man', Father would intone in solemn confirmation, 'could tell how many times the clock ticked in a year!' In an excess of that precocity that has gained me some enemies and lost me not a new friends, I sat down one night and worked out the figure. There was no doubting the pride in Father's eyes when I burst in upon him with the magic news. 'Be the livin' Christ,' he said, 'I made no mistake in calling you William after him all right!'

My light of life upon the world can scarcely have been greeted with unmitigated ecstasy. Rarely, in fact, can a child have been less wanted: Mother was forty-six, Father two years older; with eleven squalling proofs of love's old sweet song behind them, they can hardly have looked with favour upon the twelfth intruder. They would have known well the meaning of Scott Fitzgerald's line:

> This is the way the world goes,
> The rich get richer, the poor get — children!

Unbidden to the feast I may have been, but that did not in the least inhibit my insistence on being there. This insistence, though not expressed in so many words, was nonetheless abundantly clear in the screams that my outsize lungs visited upon our narrow home. To this, no fewer than three mothers would testify. They were, in order of age: my grandmother, who lived near us and was always in the house; my own mother; and a disabled sister, then twenty and from an accident of childhood condemned to walk with difficulty for the rest of her life. My coming meant one more mouth to feed, another foot upon that treadmill of unending work, and that too at a time of depression far worse than anything we know now. Yet it is a fact that, however poor the circumstances, a child once born was always welcome into such homes; was, in fact, in constant danger of being devoured with love, so surely was it the heart and centre of the house. From the very start I was enveloped in this sense of multiple possession.

From early on, I developed an incubus that was the terror of my infant life: this great swelling thing would begin to whirl and swing inside my head, it would get bigger and thicker and faster, and the whole world would be caught up in its wild and turbulent beat; then, just when it was about to burst in pieces, and me along with it, I would wake screaming and struggling to get free. I would have the whole house in a turmoil, with women shouting and running about and holy water being flung all over the place, until at last I was kissed and hugged and lulled back to sleep, and the house would settle down again into a fog of feathered nightshade.

It was in those threatened hours that my infant heart began to know of love and, though blind to all else about me, began to shape the at once imperilled and protected person I was to become — and remain all the days of my life. From then too I date a special bond I had with this disabled sister who, though as useless in the world as I, then filled so unique and necessary a purpose.

That February day in the last year of the nineteen-twenties
when I chose to be born must have been a time of hope in
Ireland. Despite the catastrophic civil war and the fratricide of
great men who should have lived to build the country, the fact is
that for the first time in centuries the resources of Ireland were
being used for genuinely Irish purposes. Arthur Griffith,
founder of Sinn Féin and apostle of national self-reliance, would
have been pleased to see his dream come true. It was but a beginning, but for increasing numbers it meant a constant job, the
start of some sort of industrial base, the fruits of a rule aimed at
strengthening the economy rather than the rape of previous centuries. The same civil war was still a burning issue, and all
through my childhood we children went up and down the street
roaring defiance at the hated 'Shinners', never for an instant
knowing, apart from familial hearsay, what our difference with
them was:

> Vote, vote, for President Cosgrave,
> Turn away Deva from the door.
> And when Deva is knocked out,
> We will all give out the shout,
> And we'll never vote for Deva any more!

President Cosgrave was W. T. Cosgrave, who for good
measure was Cork's own representative in the Dáil. He was
small and dapper, he wore a wing collar and had a trim moustache — to us the epitome of bourgeois elegance! He would
endear himself to the crowds in Patrick Street by mimicking,
badly, in a Cork accent the then current derision of De Valera's
party's electoral ploy on the price of bread: 'Feena Faul has only
one point of policy, to reduce the price of the bread — be a
heeapinny in the peeur (a halfpenny in the pair)!'

'Deva' in our song — De Valera — was a long Savonarolan
wraith who, the elders said, hated the English, and was in
cahoots with the IRA and their valkyrie chief, Mary
MacSwiney, sister of the first hunger-strike martyr, Lord Mayor
Terence MacSwiney, living symbol of the fight for freedom and
darling of our own rebel Cork. Pretend as he might, we children
knew well that under that black cloak of Dev's lurked the devil's
tail and cloven hoof; and when we sang about him it was not to
eulogise:

9

What's the news, what's the news,
De Valera pawned his shoes,
For to buy ammunition for his men.
He was coming round the corner
When he heard an eighteen-pounder
And the sly little devil ran away!

This was fun, and as children we enjoyed it, but the fact is that it was laying down a groundwork of mistrust and suspicion, which would be the main basis for the political life of Ireland in the years to come. The republican ethic — surely the most sensible basis of rule for democratic peoples — was poisoned in our young minds by the cynicism of those post-civil-war years to the point where 'republican' meant all that was retrograde, jaundiced, carping and mean. You could tell a republican by the cut of his face: pale, pious and anguished with the way things were going right! Even the comic songs had it:

Never marry a soldier, a sailor or a marine,
But marry an old Sinn Féiner with his backside painted
   green.
So right you are, right you are,
Right you are, me jolly soldiers, right you are!

When De Valera came to Cork, his precursor was Molly Owens, a great bloated model straight from Michelangelo, who ran a fruit and vegetable store at the foot of Shandon Street, where our tenement house was. Like the seafaring Gráinne O'Malley of sixteenth-century Mayo, she could have a thousand fighting men to her beck and call whenever she wanted them. She would have tar barrels burning for her hero all the way in from Blackpool, and when the parade reached Quarry Lane, bitter battlefield of the old Parnell split, the enemy would be in wait for them, hara-kiri gladiators whose passion for slaughter was compounded in equal parts of hurling, drag-hunting, bowl-playing and old family feuds — together with what small mite of national fervour might be needed to fire the incendiary mixture.

Yet despite all this, the country was settling down. The police used batons, not guns; the soldiers stayed in their barracks; the days of the Black and Tans, the informers shot in laneways, and the ambushes honoured in song and in story were over.

10

Remote from it all, living our 'lives of quiet desperation', we were becoming children of a new nation; and so when, on that spring morning that thrust me naked upon the world, my younger sister peeped across the side of the cot and cried 'He eye dee open!', what his eyes opened upon was a fractious, brawling, half-starved, wildly energetic and largely unused slum-folk born to a dawn of freedom and with the new horizons of freedom opening up. The red sandstone earth was being torn up for the foundations of a brand-new city on Guarranabraher, Garden of the Monks, atop the brow of our north-side hills. Women like my mother from the tenement rooms dreamed of such places where they would have a house of their own, a glassy palace verily — complete with lavatory, running water and a brightly polished stove. Oh, bliss were it upon that dawn to be alive — but the key to such a house was very heaven! The rotten mattresses dumped in the back lanes, the grime and soot of the open fires giving way to curtains of white lace and a green garden beyond, strange names and new places worthy of the dreams she had for us — hopes and dreams her dreamy man had filled her with before the world got him and he stopped such foolishness forever. From then on, the brawling and drunkenness would cease, the smells of wood-rot and the rot of excrescence, human and animal, the hundred Hogarthian lives crowded and packed into a small place — all that would vanish in the smell of new paint and bright linoleum, and her children would grow up clean and healthy men and women, schooled in the book-knowledge that would win an honoured place for them in this brave new world!

Week by week, Mother trudged to the City Hall to plead with weighty toadies grown big with office to get herself a notch higher on the waiting-list. She had a case: six children in two slum rooms four floors up; no light, no sanitation, no water but a single tap in the ground-floor yard, and one cracked lavatory to serve the entire house. It took time. The lists were full, there were always others who could plead a harder case. She would come back trailing her shawl then, her heart even lower — but life went on, and that insistent treadmill would not let her go.

What a life it was! Sudden, unaccountable screams by night; neighbour feuds marked by murderous savagery; the menfolk, mad with drink, stripped to the waist for single combat, brandishing cut-throats or knives to the screams of women and the lost wailing of children; the pallid and tuberculous young and the indestructible old, the hucksters and usurers and penny-policy men, the rent-collectors and pawnbrokers and fat women with fur coats who lived off the order-books of the poor, the Woodbines and snuff and orgies of flat porter from a bucket at Christmas-time, the Saturday night ruin of small solvencies, the Monday morning journey to pawn office or loan office to bring the solvency back before the next dreaded treadmill week began.

I saw it and lived it, I loved it and hated it, a stray waif set down in the midst of a mad world and set to ride its star. It was good though when the horses came up the hill, great loads piled on drays behind them, the demented drivers goading them on to gain a foothold upon the rutted road. Father, whose hero-worship of his fellow-soldiers had not abated one iota over the years, had chosen as godfather for me a near relative, Timmy Miller (affectionately known by his Irish name, Taidhgín), who had been with the cavalry in the Great War.

What the cavalry of those years meant was flogging spent mares and stallions gone beyond their best through the morasses of No Man's Land, with Big Berthas of cannon loaded up behind them — good training for the carter he was to become when he got back home to Cork. My own sense of hero-worship leaped alive when I saw him make a run at the hill atop his loaded dray: if he got a good run, they could make it to near the top; then the horses were exhausted, with the worst still to come. There was a moment of taut and murderous danger as he jumped down and was in beside them, in under them, the foaming bridles in one hand, the short whip in the other, running along in threesome to urge them on. It was a wild world then of frothing, foaming horse and man, flesh and bone and blood, of muscle and of mind, flints sparking the road under the plunging hooves, the great Clydesdales black with sweat, and veins bulging on their sides, my Ben Hur godfather under them in terror of one thing and one thing only, that they would slip and fall and bring the slim grip he had upon the world of solvency down upon the ground.

It sometimes happened. Then the horses had to be untackled, and when the bit was out and the straddle off there was no con-trolling the frightened beasts. Great hooves went flying wildly looking for a purchase upon the rutted road, and the men who came to help scattered like frightened birds as the panting giants, eyes bulging and nostrils wide with fear, lay hunched against the next assault. Sometimes, a leg was broken and the horse had to be shot. For my Flanders godfather-hero, that was the last defeat: he would stand there, lank and helpless, as the humane killer, dull muzzle to the horse's temple, made a hollow sound; and instantly the struggling creature died all over, the weight of the dray tightening upon the tangled tackle, garrotting its limbs in a dozen different places.

Looking on upon the scene would be another relative, my Uncle Johnny, who had lost a leg with the 'Munsters' in the Dardenelles. That put him out of action for good: he had no option now but to sit with his thoughts and his empty trouser-leg and cast a cold eye on life and on death, horseman pass by! He couldn't help: all he could do was pity — and what pity can be left in a man who has battered out the last of his strength in an even more senseless struggle long, long before? Such is the perversity of things that sometimes at such moments up the hill would come Dr Hearne, the Protestant bishop, a kindly man whom everyone liked but who fitted ill into this scene, murmuring words of comfort about a man's duty to his country and praised be the holy will of God! Johnny would nod in mute but furious acquiescence: Taidhgín's horses and his livelihood dead on the roadway and his own empty trouser-leg said things about the will of God that made it a very different thing in the world to which they belonged!

But life went on in our Seán O'Casey 'two-pair-back' at the top of the dark stairs. From early on I learnt to advertise my comings with loud cries to draw attention from those above; if I had to go up alone at night with no light but the cracks from under the doors, it was a testing time for young nerves. Suddenly there would be a creak and a door would open, revealing a cowering figure, more frightened, if that were possible, than I. Annie Downey kept cats that howled like wolves at night — she was coming out to find them; beside her was Miss Goggin, a porcelain doll dressed up in cretonne and smelling of old scent; and down below, Willie and wife, landlord and landlady — Good by name but bad by nature, as they called week by week for the rent, a risky business when tempers ran high and funds ran low, as they nearly always did.

Across the road in a dark hole smelling of tanned leather and burning thong-wax was a half-crippled cobbler, Dan Hurley, a

13

Rumpelstiltskin of a man, black as Hell and malevolent as the devil. He slid like an adder up and down off his cobbler's stool, and whetted his knife on a leather apron that bore the marks of a thousand cuts.

Politics, everywhere the opium of the poor, was in Ireland our constant and our delight: whatever the civil war can have done to him, the cobbler hated De Valera; and all his hunched and choking fury came to life at the sound of the execrated name. In a rage summoned from God knows what poisoned hell, he would slide from the stool when word came up the road that the Broy Harriers were coming: they were the KGB of the De Valera police. We waited in mute terror inside doors and windows then, while women gathered their children to places of safety, and the black face of the De Valera man glinted like Dracula's inside the shattered glass. Then, suddenly, as they hove in view, the glass would shatter as last and hammer came out at them, followed in hot pursuit by the twisted cobbler himself: 'Up Dibbelera, ha!' he spat like a cobra, coming at them with a frenzy wonderful in a man of his size; and the men of peace backed off, as well they might, sensing his daemonic power.

It was not uncommon on festive nights when the drink ran high, for feuding families to roar challenges at each other across the echoing lanes. 'Come out, ye creepers, if ye have the guts! Send out yeer fightin' men now!' There would be a moment of silence, then doors would burst open, and belts and sticks and pokers would go to work; to this day, if a child falls in a church, I know instantly the sound: it is Pet Horgan hitting the steps below our room, or Burly Con falling on one of the O'Connells, his harridan wife bringing up the rear to hit whatever moved when he was done.

Mother could never stand such brawling, and was quite without fear in going in to stop it. Once, at the station in Youghal, while waiting for the excursion train going back home at the end of a long day, two murderous giants fell on each other on the platform, and as the crowd fled in all directions she rushed between them and tore and held them apart with a power and strength amazing in a woman of her size. When the police came, they began to pound them and she flew at them too. It was not courage, more a primeval tigress instinct that could not bear hurt or injury to one of her own kind.

Drink was a cause of much of this, but despair with hopeless lives was greater. Proper housing, decent wages, better social conditions — all these would eventually bring change; but none would bring the changes education brought, however dimly and unconsciously at the time that was perceived.

Mother was one of the first to see it. 'Knowledge is no load', she would say; or, when the spartan Brothers did their worst in punishment and retribution: 'They're only for yeer good!' It was all to our advantage, we'd be glad of it yet; just keep to the books, get the examinations, at the end of all there would be the reward of a fine white-collar job. We did not know then the term 'white-collar' — had not yet reached such discerning heights — but we had terms of our own: we would not have to take off our coats to work; would not be out in all weathers in the muck and slush to make our way; would have a fine office 'below in Government Buildings' or 'above in Dublin', not on the docks or coal-yards where you'd surely get your death!

The mindless boredom of such white-collar jobs was as yet utterly unknown to us; the mere mention of such a thing would have been blasphemy. Get but one foot upon the ladder of success, and a whole new world would be born. If this was small ambition, and it was, it was real too: it marked that crucial point in the graph of progress when children of a new nation begin to think for the first time of finding a place in the sun; thereafter, slums and docks and coal-yards would not condemn them to capricious and vindictive destinies. A small beginning, but a beginning just the same, on the long trek out of the colonial past.

Our eldest brother was a child of that time. When, at the end of the years of study by candlelight or paraffin lamp, news came that he had got himself a place in the civil service, there was great rejoicing; he was our Moses leading us out of dark captivity in Egypt into the promised land! Soon after came even better tidings: whether from coincidence or this new claim upon official respect, when Mother next went on one of her treasure-hunts to the City Hall, she was given the keys of a new house. There was a mad splurge of buying then. New beds and bed-clothes were piled up in the hall; there was a kitchen table and new chairs of white wood; there were rolls of linoleum like liquid gold stacked against the slum-room wall.

Bill Buckley, a distant relative and a carter by trade, came to collect them, and when they were piled high upon his dray I was put up beside him — the rest of the family could walk — and we moved off, like one of those sharecropping prospectors in Steinbeck, hungry to inherit our new-found world. Atop the cart, I looked back upon the place where I was born. There was a black cat in the doorway, a sign of luck. Was the luck before us or behind? With six of us still around, there was at least a chance. And enough love and life about to make sure we took it.

2

MOTHER COURAGE

IT IS NO good my trying to do an orderly character sketch of my mother. Of all the people in my early life, she is the one I was closest to; but then — even then especially — her moods and fancies swung like the cock on the weather-vane, making it difficult if not impossible to find consistent direction. She could be ferocious in defence of her own; even more so in attacking them. I remember seeing a last come flying across the kitchen floor one day — it was aimed at her own mother, whom of course she loved; nobody was hurt, love beating rage when it came to aiming missiles like that! But such hot flushes taught one's infant mind to have a care when crossing her path. 'I'm very black', she'd say, referring to some ancient grudge where she had been wronged and would never again forgive. Years later, I was reminded of her when Brecht's Mother Courage tells her wounded son she can put his insult to use only if it breeds 'the long rage'; if not, he can go and piss it out against the wall with his last drink.

A physical sketch of Mother presents even greater problems. She was small, dumpy and fat; even as an old woman she would refer to her pot-belly in terms of a pregnancy: 'five months and five minutes'; in a word, not at all the figure of the strong woman I may give the impression of here. Her strength was entirely a matter of passion. When the spirit moved her, the single most terrifying thing about her was her scream: a truly strangled and garrotted pitch that left one in no doubt of some desperate act to follow. Nobody who heard this sound could be in any doubt of its intent: trouble was coming. Trouble invariably had some domestic cause: ingratitude, real or imagined; an excessive demand by one of the girls for some small luxury like a new coat; worst of all, because Father was concerned, an attempt on his part to conceal some small financial gain like a few shillings he

17

had won on a horse. It was tornado time then when he came home, the small woman a very valkyrie who would not rest until her wounded pride had had its fill.

Father, himself no prince of peace, would try to keep cool as long as he could, but that hot love that had fused those two together when they were young still burned, burned brightest of all when she taunted him with rejection and scorn. It was terrible when they went at each other then, my whole life sundering under the clamour of their blows. When he struck her, it made a sound like clods falling on a coffin, and I cried not from pain or fear but because the heart inside me came to pieces, as up from there tears of blood and anguish flowed. I hated him then, but hated her more for the way she made me hate him, but the bind she had on me had trapped me in her love ever before time began. The sound of my wailing would sometimes bring them to their senses and they would stop before rending each other in pieces.

Of the two, she was the more shameless in exploiting my state, blaming it all on him. She left me no option but to side with her, a deft and subtle timing of her rage, turning it in due course to the bitter sobs of the insulted and the injured, which of course she was. In the emotive terminology of our own time, she would have been a battered wife, and she and I on such occasions would have found a place of refuge in some remote hideaway free from the threat of husbands; had divorce been there, she would have had cause.

Of the two, he probably needed help and pity more — at least she had the family — but I felt no pity for him at all, only gratitude when he was gone. I would hear his slow step on the stairs, retreating, defeated, undone; later I would hear him crying, a sad and lonely sound like a hunted dog. It would be years before I began to have any real inkling of his loneliness and his plight; and only now, years later again, to feel that, in seeking his half-mite from the nothing they had, he was asking no more than the least a loving man may have.

How had the idyll of thirty years before come to such a state? The woman who dominated my childhood years kept her hair in black volcanic knots pinned up and bound to her poll to keep it out of the way. Yet that mane of hair was the sole living link between the beauty she had been and the wash-tub denizen of those later years. There is a photograph of her from that time: a

18

slim and wide-eyed beauty, long tapering fingers, a black cravat at her throat and, above, a superstructure of hair, silky crenellations of jet-black rolls framing a divinely trusting face. How did such a photograph come to exist? I take her to be about twenty-one — maybe it actually dates from her twenty-first birthday. That much fixed, one may fill in the rest: they had met and married when she was nineteen, he a mere eighteen months older. He was, she would tell us, a sight to see in his Dublin Fusiliers uniform on their wedding-day: red tunic, patent-leather belt, trousers creased to a knife-edge with a red stripe slim as a reed down each side, boots burnished to mirror the sky, black glengarry above to crown it all. There was a guard of honour with swords to make an arch for them — she never felt so proud in her life.

In later years, their marriage certificate would occasionally turn up in the house when a spring-cleaning was on, yellowed now and going to dust at the back of a forgotten drawer: 'Murphy, Kennedy: Serviceman. Buckley, Julia: X — her mark'. That was the Nazi brand upon the picture-book grandeur: fine ladies they might look, but centuries of conquest meant no education and ensured that beauty could be skin-deep, soul-deep, even celluloid-deep — but never anything more!

So she met and married her soldier-boy and lived with him for a month before following him to Queenstown harbour (now Cóbh) in Cork where he took ship with his beloved 'Dubs' for South Africa, where the white chiefs, British and Dutch, were making ready to fight the Great Boer War. The photograph, I reckon, is from two years later when she was fully twenty-one and wanted to send him a keepsake of his wild Irish rose. Not that he would have needed reminding: anyone with a pair of eyes in his head can see what he saw: youth, beauty, a strange distant steadfastness that would last the lifetime that was in store. When that war ended he came home, but only for a short time, then went off again for another seven years — this time to Egypt and the Sudan, the east and west Mediterranean, Gibraltar, Malta, Cyprus, Crete.

For her it was a time of unprecedented prosperity: she had her job in the flax mill in Blackpool, which she loved as much for the camaraderie as for the money it brought; her 'separation money', consolation prize of every soldier's grass-widow, was an added bonanza. In later years she would look back upon that time when she was briefly and incredibly a woman of means; a post-office savings book said she had all of a hundred golden guineas to her name! What was ten years of marriage without a man to that!

When he came home at last, burnt copper from the sun, she did not know him; surely to God, she said when they pointed him out to her in the march-past up the Grand Parade, *that* wasn't the boy she married ten years before? He for his part might ask, was she the girl? That was 1909. There would be no more partings, no more wars to separate them now.

The following year the first of the children, my eldest sister, was born. For a long time she was an only child: in those years of high fertility, when birth control wasn't thought of, it must have looked strange; I'm sure she often asked herself if it would stay that way. Then the floodgates opened and continued for a score of years; and by the time they were done, the days of full and plenty would never come again.

Yet I must not give the impression of an unhappy house. Crowded and chaotic, yes; occasionally frenzied, always hard-up, nonetheless it was a lively place, a place of laughter and occasional hilarity, with never a lack of food and only rarely a lack of love. Against the embattled nights there were other times when they talked quietly to each other and even touched, as they sometimes did when they thought no-one was looking. Once, I remember the two of them sitting at a table looking down at me on the floor; I can't have been much above infancy, but they must have been talking about me because when I looked up I saw the 'light upon me from my father's eyes'. If I could have prayed then, I would have prayed it would always be so, a love unspoken and all the deeper for that. But it wasn't, and as I grew up and the years of infancy passed by, the other, harsher side emerged and eventually took over, until in the end there seemed to be nothing else but that at all.

It was in those later years Mother began to turn into the woman I knew — strong, resolute, inexhaustible, caring for each of us as if we were an only child, proud of our progress, tireless in advancing it, ruddy with work, a fireball of life flinging out sparks of light and hope and occasional fury to make a new world for us all. She watched over us like a tigress then and, whether in fear or love, in anger at being wronged by her or in terror of her ever being taken away, she bound us to her with a desperate and beleaguered love. When in those times things got the upper hand of her and she threatened 'to go down and throw myself in the river', child and all as I was I feared she would do it. The river was near —I could see her as I had seen others, the hooks grappling at her loose and sagging clothes, her hair flowing like weir-grass in the tide. Or again, drowsy with the smell of incense in the church, I would be struck by a sudden sense of grief as I pictured her dead, shut up in a coffin and buried in a dark hole all alone where I could not be with her. At times like that I knew that life could never hurt me except through her; and neither loss nor injury nor any deprivation at all could ever touch me as long as she was there. She could not, I then thought, ever die; how could she when she controlled my whole surrounding world, and neither God nor man nor any living thing could prevail against her all-abundant will?

All through her life, the part of it we knew, Mother was a paragon of abstemious morality. In this she was no different from the other women about the place who neither drank nor smoked nor did anything contrary to the rigid mores of their time. This was communicated to us in the most subtle yet pene-trating way: we were led to believe that such transgressions were as much in the category of sin as of bad habit, a distinction of some potency when you remembered how hugely sin bulked in our darksome penitential lives!

Smoking came first in the order of depravity. Whoever smoked showed early signs of moral decay; hence we took the precaution, if we were so inclined, of locking ourselves (or so we thought) into the tiny toilet where we could blow the smoke out through the window set high up in the wall, by standing tip-toe on the lavatory bowl. Virtue is its own reward and vice its nemesis, and one day she came bursting through the 'bolted' door at the sight of the smoke trailing happily skywards outside. In the panic, the smoke went down the trapped miscreant's wind-pipe, half choking him and bringing on a paroxysm that made him slip from his perch into the bowl below, where his two legs stuck fast as a pheasant in a field, ripe for the cockshot. Her attitude in this was only partly economic: a packet of Woodbines meant twopence, the wanton waste of the price of a pint of milk or a loaf of bread; but the moral factor was far stronger. Smoking betokened young vice and an idleness of mind abhorrent to her sense of industry.

21

She could be quite violent about it. One Christmas Eve, we were coming home from town, laden with the festive provisions. These included a goose, which I had grasped under my overcoat, its plucked neck come loose and dangling through a hole in my pocket; and a bottle of raspberry cordial, treat of treats for us children on Christmas Day. My brother who was with me had managed to sneak off when she wasn't looking and buy a double Woodbine for furtive and covert use by us boys throughout the holy season. But we had forgotten the matches. We could not risk taking hers: if she caught us, the secret was out. The swinging goose-neck and the bottle of cordial had my whole attention, when I suddenly remembered this fact.

'Jasus,' I said, in terms that may surprise the genteel, coming from a ten-year-old but, believe me, were quite normal in our state then, 'Jasus, we forgot the fuckin' matches!'

She swung round from where she was walking a few feet ahead, fire-daggers in her eyes. *What did you say?*

My brother was quick to sight the danger. 'He only said, "Jamus, we forgot the Friendly matches".'

It was a feat of brilliant improvisation. His name was James; we called him Jim; very occasionally the Irish form, Séamus; never, never in any circumstances at all, the extraordinary thing he called himself now. And Friendly was — still is — the brand name of the household matches of that time. But in his haste to improvise he had forgotten one thing: if we had forgotten the matches, then what in the first place were the matches for?

She dragged us into a nearby store whose owner she knew and could trust to keep secret the ensuing flagellation. Seeing her drift, I made a dash for it, but the goose-neck got me between the legs and, trying to get free, I let go the bottle of raspberry, which crashed in smidereens on the stone floor. Her rage was up now but her hands were full, so she drew a kick at me, whereupon her foot slipped on the raspberried floor and down she came in the pool of moral turpitude that would guarantee us a very merry Christmas indeed!

That was all because of a packet of cigarettes; in her scale of values, drink was infinitely worse. Ruin and perdition were the deserts of those who drank; never in those days would a drop pass her own lips at all! In summer, when we went on excursions to the seaside, she would dress up in her best — a new hat and a coat with a fox fur for her shoulders — and spend the day bent

22

over a twig fire on the strand, feeding us tea and sand-sandwiches until it was time to go back home.

Father would be prowling about waiting for her to finish up and come with him to the local where on this one day he could dream of the beauty she had been, fine and mighty in her rig-out, like a true-born dame — or that girl in the old photo long ago! Eventually, when he got her there, she would consent to go in, but only to the 'snug', where she would not be seen by the common crowd. Her single 'medium' on that day would have been a scandal for us to see from which she could never again adjure us against the cursed drink. The trouble was she had Father trapped in this scheme of things, and once, after our eldest brother had got his highly respected job in the civil service, he arrived home plastered with him one night, arms about each other and singing and muttering maudlin mutual affections.

'Go on,' she railed when she got him in, 'lead him astray like yourself! You'll have the unfortunate child as bad as yourself by the time you're done!' The 'unfortunate child' sensibly judged it better to remain silent, leaving their defence to the more seasoned soldier. Father pulled himself up with great dignity and swore that as God was his judge, 'the boy had only a bottle of Bass!'

When at the end of all this Father died, and the last embers of the band-box love affair were quenched, she was free to give her whole attention to us children. We were no longer children by then, but were still helpless against her forays — and were expected to reciprocate in every particular her sense of total dedication. Girl-friends she resented as if they were raging predators; talk of marriage, when it came, was the ultimate betrayal, a reneging on the lifelong hold she had upon us. This attitude of exclusive possession would be communicated in sulks and silences, in sudden fierce hints of deception and flashes of wounded indignation: a man could, we would be told, have several wives but only one mother (one wondered at the sudden death of the marriage vows — not surprising, however, since they could be no match for a mother's love!) For a woman not notably given to poetry — or any other form of reading either, apart from the 'Deaths' column in the *Evening Echo* — she would suddenly dig up the most alarming and macabre verses, mostly from Father's long-forgotten wars:

Break the news to Mother,
Tell her there's no-one other,
There's no-one else but Mother
No matter where you go.

We squirmed and died at such shameless press-ganging on
our affections, but that did not put her off. Death was a real
winner, its dark muse quick to her lips whenever any of us
attempted a getaway:

A mother's love is a blessing, no matter where you go,
Keep her while she's living, you'll miss her when she's
      gone;
Love her as in childhood though she be old and grey,
For you'll never miss your mother's love till she's buried
      beneath the clay!

Our younger sister had developed a certain armour against
this, and gave us boys great moral support at such moments of
long-tentacled possessiveness. She lived at home with her and
was well aware of the speed with which her moods of sepulchral
gravity could alternate with moods of wild hilarity and
laughter. Mother had great reams of obituary verse by heart,
culled mostly from the *Echo*; these were reduced to instant
ridicule as 'the vayrce'. Against this apostasy Mother had no
defence but to hurl back mockingly that 'Ye'd never know
who'd be mocking yeer own child yet!' Such encounters invariably ended in the grim assurance that 'Them is gone is
better off!' Whereat our sister, not to be outdone, would put on
the tragic mode and moan in mimicry, 'I wish I was stretched
outside in Douglas!' (Douglas Cemetery was where Father had
been buried.)

Yet all the same she was getting old, and the frequency of such
lugubrious utterance told its tale. She slept less, a habit not un-
connected with the fact that our brother was a bus-conductor
and had to be out at all hours to take the first service to the
country fairs. He would fall into bed at midnight, pole-axed
with exhaustion, leaving strict orders to us all to get him up in
time. We all promptly forgot — but her. Then out of the depths
of our slumbers the bus would shatter us awake as it came
throbbing and shuddering up the road. Everyone in the street,
not to mind the house, was shaken to life, all except him; having

24

safely delegated the task of waking him, he could sleep soundly on. Then all of a sudden the house became a wild circus, with 'Jesus, Jesus' being imprecated from heaven to get him up: 'He's here, he's here, get him up for Jesus' sake, he'll be sacked!' This was a cataclysm of such staggering magnitude that truly, it was no joke, it would be the bitter ruin of us all! Through the fog of sleep and shattered dreams, dark memories of life on the dole or death in pagan England would stir the deepest sleep; the whole house would be awake, with lights and shouts and windows being flung up and down, while the leviathan throbbed and trembled at the door, even then failing to get our sleeper awake. Eventually he would come to, and by some hand unknown to himself or us get into his clothes, and at last be bundled out into the raw air, bread and rashers and boiling tea being flung after him — whereat the leviathan would rattle and chain-saw its way up the street again, to the cursing of Billy Lynch, the driver, upon all the curse-o'-God snoring mates the world had ever known!

After that, it was like the knocking at the gate in *Macbeth* — Duncan murdered, the deed done, we could all go back to sleep again.

We all did — except her. The habit of dawn-rising that she had had from the flax-mill days had never really left her, but with age and the labour of years it had taken its toll, mostly in a kind of moping vacancy wherein she saw what went on about her but only vaguely took it in. I was the last of the brood, and when I came home from school in the evenings, she would be sitting at the window, glazed eyes looking out for the familiar faces and the familiar footfalls that timed her every day. No-one new was coming home now any more: the tide had gone out and would not be back again in her time. Gone now were the days of the zinc tub full of clothes in the middle of the kitchen floor and the strong arms kneading them; gone the summer days when the winter blankets were stripped down and washed and hung out on the line to dry.

It's as she was at that time that I best remember her, midway between the youth I never knew and the age that came down like a cloud — her brood still to forage for, her truculence and embattlement more than a match for the insult of a life she had to live. Not in the smallest particular would she betray one iota of that life — nor dared any of us boys or girls do so either. We had good reason to be afraid of her then, her rage quick and her congealed strength quicker — but stronger than all was the strength of her fidelity to each and every one of us, especially when we were down.

Sometimes, in those last years, I would come upon her by accident — sitting or shuffling about in a half-trance, eyes glued to the paper but not seeing it, praying fitfully, moving the table-things from place to place. One might detect in that ineffectual mobility the early signs of arterial decay — a body exhausted, harnessed to a will that was not. To the mute accompaniment of her thoughts and sayings, daily regurgitated and recycled, I, being alone now to hear them, would become bored to distraction by their sameness; as often as not, I fell asleep at the table as she talked, and when I woke, she'd be still there at the window, watching the world go by, knowing as I think all sentient creatures one day must know that this time of later peace would not come by again.

Sometimes, later in the night, we would sit around the fire, and our sister, as much from idleness as for any other reason, would begin to comb her hair; the long tresses fell about her shoulders just as they must have done for that girl in the photograph, silken, shining and still quite remarkably black. She would purr audibly at the unaccustomed care: 'Amn't I the nice little girl, now!' Her moods were calmer, she often mentioned death: emigration was another great favourite; both figured in her even-then growing repertoire of songs. These seemed to flood back as the tide went out, Famine-paeans of God-awful calamity, with half the neighbours weeping at a party by the time she'd done:

> Oh, look at the big ship a-sailing,
> It is bound for some far distant shore;
> And listen to the cries and the wailing
> For the land they will never see more.
> Some cry for their wives and their childring [!]
> And more for their sweethearts at home,
> For no more they'll return to old Ireland,
> The loved land, the Irishman's home.

I am not at all certain that these masochistic celebrations didn't affect my own view of the world, which, though normally calm, balanced and well ordered, can at times lurch into sudden

26

alarming bouts of tearfulness. But as she grew older she became more assertive too, and never tired of talking about her personal achievement in bringing us up against the odds. Once this started, there was no stopping her; just try — and we did — and the whole world would know.

What was it they were ashamed of? What were they trying to hide? That their mother was illiterate? Well, she was! That she couldn't write her name? Well, she couldn't! Child of the slums and the sweat-labour of the flax mills, that's what she was! And proud of it too, as why should she not — up at dawn at the age of ten and out to earn her bread from the eye of evil: small wonder she'd shout, her man gone and her family reared — why shouldn't she shout at the end of her days!

The day I was married it all came together. There was wine, an unaccustomed beverage; furthermore, it was white — what harm was that, coloured water really, to be drunk by the gallon with no effect! I could see it all coming, so could the others, but we seemed powerless to act.

Inevitably, sooner or later, someone began to sing; it was *Oh, My Beloved Father* — there is a devilish connivance in such things. Suddenly, at the mention of Father, she was up and away. From my place at the table, I could hear her cut loose from the arresting hands. It was their father would be proud of them this blessed day, a man with nothing but his four bones, not like the grandees now about her — why wouldn't she shout, who was going to stop her, was it of their mother they were ashamed! . . .

Coward that I am, I fled the scene and made for the bar but could hear her as I went down the stairs. By then, she was in full flight, had burst into song herself, a song of Father's from one of the old wars:

> All around the shanty table,
> Sitting with a social few,
> Nothing else could be more pleasant
> Than those few hours I spent with you.
>
> Happy are we all together,
> Happy are we one and all,
> That we may live a life of pleasure,
> That we may rise and never fall!

It was October, the end of the month; the first frost was edging the leaves. By six o'clock it was dusk, and after I had got safely away I happened to be walking with my new wife through the churchyard of the tourist village where we were to stay. It occurred to me that only some preternatural love of death and disaster could have brought me to such a place on my wedding day! But as I walked about amidst the old stones, with the moss of ages blurring the forgotten names, her wild and raucous voice came alive inside me.

Yes, she was all she said — common and illiterate, a noisy and truculent old woman with a garrulous pride in her own small gains; she was high because she knew no better, and right now was probably sleeping it off somewhere in the full view of everyone, having exhausted herself with her passion for grief and her even more grievous passion for gaiety. Yet it was none of those petty things that was in my heart that October night, but at long last the fear with which she had held me ever since the day I was born: the fear of her footfall dying upon the world, dying like the leaves of summer now shrunk and withered on the ground. I knew then that nothing she ever did to make me hate her could stop me loving her; and I knew that when she went, nothing would ever fill the place she held for me in the world.

She had her wish at last: her four sons did indeed carry her coffin down 'Evergreen': she couldn't be dead soon enough to cash in that cheque upon our love! I was one of the four, the last — undoubtedly a mistake. For me, for her too I hope, it was a most rewarding folly.

3

THE SAXON SHILLING

A NY ACCOUNT of Father has to begin and end by saying that he was a soldier. His soldiering life began at the age of nineteen, went on through two wars and several campaigns throughout the next twenty-one years, and when at last he came home to settle down after it all, he went on to spend the rest of his life talking about his soldiering days.

The soldier in him came out in the manner of his dress: smart and razor-sharp, clipped moustache and creased hair, trousers pressed to a knife-edge, shoes burnished to mirror the sky. This was neither customary nor inherited — just one more example of a habit learnt young. During a regimental parade in South Africa at the start of the Boer War, he had 'taken the stick': a token white baton awarded to the smartest soldier in the regiment. That earned him the further reward of being made batman to the regimental commander, Lord Lonsdale, friend and coeval of the Churchills, Haldane, Julian Amery and the other colonial élite. There can be little doubt that such high-flying company, even in a time of war, had profound effects upon the boy.

Years later, when all his wars were over and times were bad, his one good suit and pair of shoes would go off to the pawn on Monday morning, our wherewithal for the coming week; when they were redeemed the following Saturday he would set about them with iron and steam-cloth, while the shoes, already perfect to my eyes, would be tinted with marker-ink to bring up the ruby sheen, and polished yet again to make them a very sight to see. By Sunday, when he dressed up, with starched shirt and brown 'couteau' hat, he looked the picture of the well-dressed man: if there were a 'stick' going, he would have won it by a street!

We were all proud of him then, and loved to be seen with him when he went down town to meet his friends. It was a brief return to parade-ground glory — alas, to be bundled away again on Monday morning and left to moulder in the mothballs till the next Saturday's pay-packet could get them out again.

This instinct for perfection could take on less personal forms. Once, when the family went on a holiday to a bungalow in Cross-haven at the mouth of Cork harbour, he stayed at home alone all week long, and when we came back, the house was gleaming: floorboards scrubbed, walls washed down, garden trimmed and barbered as if it were some corner of Titania's Palace.

The story of how he came to be a soldier in the first place says a great deal about his explosive nature. He had, it seems, some sort of menial job, but being young, hot-tempered and quick to quarrel, he fell foul of the boss and lost it; he threatened then to run away from home, but his mother, knowing the fiery particle she had, stripped him of his clothes and physically tied him to the leg of the bed. This only served to strengthen further his resolve to get away, which he did, tearing off his bonds and getting his legs into the sleeves of an old cardigan, which served as a makeshift trousers. In this strange garb he presented himself to the recruiting sergeant of the Dublin Fusiliers who, though Father was below the accepted recruiting age, was in no mood to question the willingness of young and able-bodied Irishmen to press themselves into Her Majesty's service on the eve of the Boer War.

So it was that the half-naked 'Mad Sweeney' from Ireland went into the service of Sir Redvers Butler, Lord Roberts, and Kitchener of Khartoum to help them win and hold the gold-rich lands north of Pretoria and the Transvaal.

The teenage boy out from the town of Cork in southern Ireland had probably never heard of any of them — to say nothing of their enemies, Paul Kruger and Kronje, Louis Botha and Jan Smuts; and almost certainly had not the slightest notion of what it was all about; but the six-week voyage on a troop-ship was long enough to cut the cord of memory and launch him headlong into the new colonial world. It was the world of Kipling and the gods of Empire, of bravery and regimental loyalty — and the mad and mindless regimental ballads that served to buttress it:

> They're as brave, they're as bold,
> As the armoured knights of old.

30

'Hats off to them', we must exclaim!
For in our darkest hour of need
'Twas they helped us to succeed
For the honour of old England's name!

Lacking any sort of education at home, certainly lacking it in any national sense, they were ripe for exploitation, cunningly instilled as loyalty to regimental tradition. The 'Dubs' had, they were told, a proud and honoured history: away back in the Crimean war hadn't they sung of them:

Devils they, not mortal men, the Russian general swore,
As we tore them off the Alma Heights in September '54.

This was a sentiment which was soon to have its Boer War equivalent:

Bravely fought upon the Glencoe Heights,
Put five thousand crafty Boers to flight,
It was a grand, a glorious sight —
Bravo, the Dublin Fusiliers!

All this became fused in Father's mind with the adventures of war and the stimulus of new places; and though in other respects a man of sceptical mind, he never recovered from that early brainwashing. Like the good player who will always love the team he played with when young, he loved the 'Dubs' to his dying day, and could hardly contain his tears when reciting their jingoistic rhyming:

We drink tonight because we are so jolly,
We drink tonight to Buller, White and Colley,
Somebody gave the toast, to every man's delight.
And here's to old Buller and long may he reign,
And that's why we drink tonight!

It was this Buller, hero of the relief of Ladysmith, who had himself been relieved of his command by Lord Roberts when the British at last realised that the Boers, for all the colonial imputations of laziness, slovenliness, backwardness and narrow-mindedness, did indeed mean business.

The Pretoria command sent an armoured train north daily into the troubled Uitlanders' territory, to advise the Boers of their presence and reassure their own beleaguered settlers that the British lion was very much there. But such armed intrusion into their own lands proved too much for the Boers to bear, and one day a commando fell upon it and made the metal-plated wagons, which were open on top, a soft and murderous target. The company commander, Julian Amery, was wounded in the attack, and the whole convoy would have been massacred but for the courage and decisiveness of a young journalist reporting the war for his paper back in London and who, against orders, had accompanied the train that day. It so happened that this young man had been the guest of Father's Lord Lonsdale the night before, and he had actually served him at table. The wreck of the armoured train made headlines in all the South African and British papers, and right up to the time he died, Father would tell with pride how he had picked up the *Capetown News* the following day and saw the picture of the young hero on its front page. His name was Winston Churchill.

No sooner was he back from fighting the Boers just after the turn of the century than he was off again, this time to the northern end of the continent: Egypt, the Sudan, and all the outposts of the Mediterranean: Gibraltar, Malta, Cyprus, Crete.

By then he was well married — it was the time of that studio photograph — but nine years was a long time to be away, the lost and forgotten life of a soldier of fortune thousands of miles from home, the back-streets of Valletta in Malta and Heraklion in Crete, of Alexandria, Aden and Cairo his familiar, rather than the streets of Cork he had left behind long, long ago. An Alexandria church heard the voices of the Dublin Fusiliers explode in the chorus of a hymn one Christmas Eve: 'Oh, Parnellites, Oh, Parnellites' instead of the 'Oh, Paradise, Oh, Paradise' they were meant to sing; the mile swim from Vincent's Bridge to Water Street in the Lee in Cork became seven miles in the tepid waters of midsummer Malta.

By the time his African and Mediterranean days were done, Bismarck had left the legacy of a new united Germany, big and strong enough to resent being pushed around in the world. That was 1914, and though he was no longer young, no longer the wild Irish boy trussed up in his mother's cardigan and glad of the 'Saxon shilling' to get him out, he was nothing but a soldier of fortune now, and off he went again. What matter that by now he had had all the war and hero-worship he wanted; what matter

32

that he had a family at home he wanted to be with — the 'Dubs' were in his blood, enlistment was as much a matter of routine as of choice. Away he went, this time to Flanders and the mud of No Man's Land. The regimental rhymers were still active as they had always been:

> They may build their ships, my lads,
> Think they know the game,
> But they can't build the boys of the Bulldog Breed
> That made old England's name!

But some new awareness of the plunder of gullible loyalties would make him add his own acidulous reprise:

> Send out your mother, your sweetheart or your brother —
> But for Christ's sake don't send me!

Yet for all its death and maiming, the mud and swamps and squalor, it was still possible to dream of the future for which they were fighting — that 'world fit for heroes to live in' that Lloyd George so cunningly held out. What matter if it should turn out to be the same slums and hunger and love on the dole; if the children who were lucky got to manhood and those who weren't were luckier still because they avoided what coming to manhood meant; if the young and the lovely grew old and ugly before their time, and if spirited and comely girls became gnarled harridans fighting their menfolk for the bread and board that was their sole care — in those years of the maiming and misery of No Man's Land, hope sprang eternal, a dim rush-light to relieve the horror of their living days.

When eventually he came back from it all, was finally and ter-minally demobbed, his future, like his past, was behind him. By then, there was something else to engage people's minds in Ireland. That year, 1919, was the year of the Sinn Féin landslide; the blood-sacrifice of 1916 had swept the ethic of empire aside, the era of polite politics was over, the physical force men made the running from then on. Yeats, an unlikely balladeer, put it well:

> Oh, but we talked at large before
> The sixteen men were shot,
> But who can talk of give and take
> What should be and what not
> While those dead men are loitering there
> To stir the boiling pot?

In the years that followed, the heroes of song and story were not the heroes of the Marne, Ypres and the Somme, but the men of Kilmichael and Crossbarry, small but strategic ambushes aimed at paralysing the occupying forces, the forerunner of all subsequent guerrilla war. And the honoured names were not Haig or French or Sir Ian Hamilton — who, it was now coming out, had sent thousands of Irishmen to suicidal deaths in the tactical madness of the Dardenelles — but men of sterling personal bravery who did the fighting themselves: Michael Collins and Tom Barry, Ernie O'Malley, Seán Tracey and Dan Breen. Those were the new names, this the new Ireland, those the new heroes everyone looked up to. Soon, the red tunic of the Dublin Fusiliers was seen in the streets no more, the very name of the Irish regiments dared scarcely be mentioned; and with them perished the whole colonial ethic, its wars seen now for what they really were: meaningless fights in another nation's interest for which Father and his likes were mere cannon-fodder, and all for the pension of ten shillings a week if you lived or twenty-six and eightpence if you died — a fine memento for the housefuls of orphans left behind.

It was all over now, for Father and the rest of them, the 'Munsters' and 'Dubs', the Connaught Rangers and Leinster Rifles — they could all hang up their boots and their rifles now, there would be no more wars for them to fight any more.

He got a job as a railway porter. It wasn't much, but it was better than selling card-matches outside theatres like many another who came back to that 'land fit for heroes'. 'There's a picture!', he'd sometimes say, holding up his fully stamped insurance card to our uncomprehending eyes. Even racked with chronic rheumatic pain, which was the trenches' legacy, and the bronchitis turned to tuberculosis which eventually got him, he never missed a day's work throughout all those years. 'Unless they shoot us, we Dublin Fusiliers refuse to die!'

It was a brave boast: but the brave die hardest of all. That winter he became quieter and more reflective; thinner and slighter too, if such a thing were possible, though none of us noticed that at the time. I marched beside him at that year's Poppy Day parade — he still turned out in the creased trousers and burnished shoes — but there was not much talk about the war, their war, any more. By then, another one was raging, this time in the slush and mud of Stalingrad; the flower of Europe's youth was dying once again, as the flower of theirs had died in Flanders and No Man's Land.

A little while before, with Rommel at his height in the North African desert and Montgomery and his Desert Rats not yet caught up with him, there was talk of an invasion of Ireland. Our eldest brother, child of the new generation, sometimes playfully taunted him with memories of the old brigade: 'I suppose,' he'd say, 'if the British were to invade us tomorrow, the 'Dubs' would be out there to help them?' He would grab the sweeping-brush and with mad fire in his eyes ram its handle bayonet-wise against the kitchen wall: 'By Jasus then and we would not!' he'd roar. 'The Dubs were Irish and we'd be out to face them as we faced the Prussian bastards in Flanders and the Somme!'

When the parade was over that year, he took off his regimental medals — the Mons Star, the Ypres Cross, the Medal for Honour and Bravery, and the one for long service and good conduct — and put them away with the Flanders poppy in their wooden box. He would not take them out again. His cough got worse as winter thickened; the fool of a panel doctor, who had been feeding him war-talk when he might have been giving him some proper medicine, diagnosed rheumatism when even a child could see it was worse, and sent him off to hospital to rest.

That was the last humiliation. The hospital was the county home — it was called the Union, with all that word connoted of the Poor Law mind. By day the 'paupers' — there was no mincing words in those days — lumbered about the wards in hobnailed boots, their thick homespuns the very epitome of destitution; at night when the lights went out, an old man in the bed beside him jabbered in senile decay into the small hours. It was not an end the boy who had 'taken the stick' with the 'Dubs' in Africa had dreamed about.

Coming up to the New Year, my brothers went to see him; they brought him a pack of Guinness to help pass the time. When they were finished they asked what they should do with the empties; he said nothing but jumped out of bed and sent them flying down into the cobbled yard. There was a glasshouse there where by day the 'paupers' did occupational work; the missiles went shattering through its glass roof. The following day he was discharged, his 'rheumatism' suddenly and miraculously cured!

I sometimes think about that New Year night, the last he

would see on earth. Had he come to realise that he had not long to go? That crashing glass in a poorhouse yard — what was it saying? That they would not take this son of fire alive? It was his last fling, he would not come again.

He had not been to Mass for a long time and had long ago given up confession and all that: so, in the theology of his time, he was a lost soul, dead to God and the church; yet I pray for him now all the time, knowing that a good man is good despite those things, and that his rage at dying was the rage of Dylan Thomas — at being robbed of a life he had once loved and of a gift he would have made more of if only he had been given half a chance:

> And you, my father, there on the sad height,
> Curse, bless me now with your fierce tears, I pray,
> Do not go gentle into that good-night.
> Rage, rage against the dying of the light,
> Do not go gentle into that good-night.

We buried him in the new cemetery in Douglas, out on the edge of town. He was with the other old soldiers there — that he would have liked.

There is a green hill above the place with a copse of beech on top, and in the evening great flocks of birds gather there to make a fine, dusky sound. It is a far cry from the poppy-fields of Mons and farther still from the pampas-grass and the broad veldt of Paul Kruger's Transvaal — in any of which places he might have laid his bones. There is a stone over his grave with nothing but his name. If it were bigger and we had known it, we might have added a line from Siegfried Sassoon: 'Look up, and swear by the slain of Flanders that you will not forget.' I do not think we will.

36

4

'O DEATH, WHERE IS THY STING?'

IF, WITH ALL this talk of death and dying, I am giving the impression that death itself was exclusively an occasion for grief, I am wrong: all three — birth, death and marriage — though different in our emotional scale could all be occasions, if not exactly for joy, at least for communal celebration. Given the prevailing fertility, birth was commonest: there was always a party when a child was born, my own birth being celebrated with a tierce of stout — small wonder I can sing like a lark to this day!

Marriage, being exclusively within our own class, had to be funded from already non-existent funds; yet I never remember a marriage that wasn't a lively affair, with singing and dancing until all hours — till the bride and groom came home in fact after their half-day honeymoon!

But death was the real bonanza. The money came in the form of insurance policies that were cashed in like dockets on the Grand National once the death certificate was signed. It was in fact the only substantial cash most families would ever have. Naturally it brought on great splurges of buying — new coats and shoes for the children, fresh lino for the kitchen floor, nights of endless drinking for as long as the proceeds of the penny policies might last. It was nothing at all for the whole house to be in on it — indeed, it was thought a slight upon a family elder to die without all the close relatives having a policy on his life. It is easy to see how this could act as a palliative against grief; what is more, it was instantaneous in that the insurance man was always there amongst the mourners on the night of the removal, and was able to pay an advance in real cash to get the ball rolling.

It was the tradition for everyone, even the children, to come to the dead-room; there was always a grand eerie feeling in there, white linen and wax candles, and the dead person whom we knew miraculously become someone or something else we did not know at all. When night fell there would be talk of ghosts. In the lamp-lit gloom they took on an alarming proximity; the rooms were full of them, and anything in white was sure to possess deathly powers.

It could have real dimensions: Will Mackesy lived up the street and collected pig-waste from house to house; we all knew him and knew he was no ghost but a poor misshapen Quasimodo whom we mocked cruelly when we got him at a safe distance. But when there was a death and night fell, he became the realest ghost you ever saw as he lurked in dark corners and wreaked terrible vengeance on us by plunging after us with great claws in the darkness, his unlaced boots clattering on the cobbles as he came.

To top it all, wasn't the devil himself seen in person then in Gurranabraher! Mother said it was a warning and a judgement on the people who lived up there — mothers of families with nothing better to do than waste their money on fags! Why wouldn't the devil take up with them, wasn't he among his own! So the priest went up, bell, book and candle, to exorcise him; but it was to no avail because he was back as large as life every time Bela Lugosi's *Dracula* came on in the local hall. A tomcat howling at night or a dog baying at the moon became the 'banshee', while we had a wholly personal ghost in our house, 'the dead nun', with an image so unearthly that she outran all screen ghosts for terror. At sight of her — and, once night was down, she was seen often — our sister would fling herself bodily from wherever she was, including down the stairs, to get out of her way!

With characteristic wile, Mother insisted in the midst of all this that there were no ghosts, only the Holy Ghost. This achieved two things: it gave us the courage to face upstairs without a candle, and was also a sly line on Christian doctrine. But Father ballsed it all up one night when he came in and said he had shot a ghost in Africa, one with a big black dog on a lead, and when the ghost stumbled and fell away into the night he dragged the dog howling behind him with a sound so terrible that he couldn't tell whether it was the dog or the ghost he had hit; then he began to blubber about 'some poor bastard of a kaffir out for a walk with his dog, all dressed up in white like

Gungha Din' — whereat Mother gave him a look fit to kill which shut him up for good.

But we didn't much need these invented ghosts; real death was commonplace enough. There were always Tiny Tims pining away in love and squalor, and the grim spectacle of Dostoievsky's dying mother spouting phthisic blood on the Nevsky Prospect as her children beg kopeks to the rhythm of the tambourine would have been no great news to us: the only difference was perhaps that in our ignorance we found more bizarre ways for dying.

Bad food, or no food at all; damp and fetid rooms; work-places that were nearer death-traps — all these got short shrift in our scale of death-causes; yet a dip out of season flouted the incantatory 'April, May, keep out of the say', and brought on a hasty end. Tuberculosis, a reasonably humane killer, was never referred to as such, rather was someone 'in bad health', 'in a decline', 'had outgrown his strength'. A 'growth' or 'something inwardly' were euphemisms for cancer, while 'a knot in the guts' and 'a stoppage of water' were well-attested ways to an early end.

And on one occasion, when Mother asked how a close relative had died, she was given an instant and knowledgeable diagnosis: 'Tripe she ate last night, Julie girl, and she's paying for it this mornin'!'

The prevailing mood in all this was resignation; acceptance of 'the holy will of God', however blasphemous of the Christian case, was yet a constant source of solace in times of trouble. What was impressive was the calm, sometimes gaiety even, with which death was faced: 'Baby' Mooney, in the last throes of TB, insisted on getting into a white dress to 'bring her colour up'; Mary Mullins asked for her man when the end was near, sat up in the bed and sang *The Old Rustic Bridge by the Mill*, then fell back on the pillow and died. Grief and song often mixed dangerously like that, leaving the bereaved grievously balanced in between.

The 'wake' could be, often was, as much an occasion for celebration as for mourning. Incredible though it may seem, I remember as many wakes that ended with singing as with crying — including the one at which Mother called the assembled mourners to order with the somewhat unusual request: 'Order now for meself, me sister-in-law is after dyin'!'

Our elder sister knew a lot about death and dying and would gladly face into any sick-room where it was. Having been at death's door herself as a child she undoubtedly retained from that time some memory of its peril. She had fallen down the steps at school at the age of five, and the two years of surgery that followed left her gravely disabled, with one leg several inches shorter than the other, which was how she was by the time I came on the scene several years later. She had gone to Lourdes on a parish pilgrimage at the age of seventeen and while there, the story goes, a lady all dressed in white came up the dormitory floor towards her one night. She had been crying, and this lady touched her and said: 'Child, you'll cry now no more!' No-one ever said this was the Blessed Virgin, but it was what we all instinctively believed. Whoever it was — if indeed it happened at all — it is a fact that she left the crutches with which she had walked up to that time behind in Lourdes; by the time I came along, some years later, she had learnt to walk, if badly, without external aid.

This early accident and the subsequent impairment marked her out as someone exceptional in the street. For others it might have meant a lifetime as an invalid, probably in a wheelchair, but quite the opposite happened with her: the disablement, so far from restraining her, actually put her in the limelight. She became known to everyone and was loved by most, not least the sick and dying whom she would nurse with a truly saintly dedication.

That was one side of her. The other was the changeling, the wicked fairy, touched with a mischief and madness that often set fire to our dull lives. She had a sewing-machine that rattled away like a steam engine into the small hours. She became a well-known fortune-teller, which meant that there was always a teapot ready on the hob. One minute she was out on her mercy missions, the next she'd have the tea-leaves swirling in a cup to invoke some god or devil to get a neighbour-girl a man. She throve on this oscillation between living and dying, serving both equally out of seemingly inexhaustible reserves of strength. Her own ailment undoubtedly helped, if that is the word.

Occasionally still her injured hip burst out in appalling bouts of ulceration that could be relieved, such was the barbarous medicine of the time, only with boiling bread-poultices! Screaming was normal in our life, but I cannot recall ever hearing anything more than a stifled moan as this living torture went on. But her powers of recovery were remarkable, and her personal courage in pain must have been a factor when painful nursing of others had to be done. It also led to a desperate prayerfulness, quite close to real sanctity, I am sure of that, though her subsequent fits of fury-cum-gaiety ensured that it would never be taken to extremes.

The Lourdes pilgrimage had been led by the Dominicans, in whose choir she was a leading light; this and the presence of some of the younger and more handsome priests with whom she and her palmist-and-tea-leaf friends could flirt covertly, priestly celibacy in those days being quite infrangible, made the church on Pope's Quay a most attractive place! This ennoblement of spirit did not at all affect their habit of referring to more available lovers in the most opprobious terms, 'John Jasus' and 'Anti-Christ' being particular favourites.

Love talk was also song time: picture the racket when her coterie of friends got going, His Master's Voice on the rickety table, the wax records scraping away with 'Streetsinger' Arthur Tracey, Nelson Eddy and Jeanette MacDonald, Tauber, Paul Robeson — and John McCormack, to cap it all, sobbing his heart out for Sweet Alice Benbolt who must have died all of a thousand times while the love-and-fortunes routine went on.

The sewing machine was an investment, which was meant to make money, but how could it when everyone who came stayed. The house was always full: mothers with daughters, sisters with pals; patterns, lengths and rolls of cloth, half-made coats and tacked-up dresses; costumes, curtains, cretonnes, organdies, silks, all waiting their turn on the clackety-clack machine to be alchemised, when the mood eventually took her, into embroidered gold! The visiting hopefuls sat around rapt in wonder at the tidings the tea-leaves brought: 'You'll be going on a journey'; 'There's a long walk between trees and water!'; 'There's a surprise in store!'; 'There'll be a stranger in the house!' And finally — always — 'There's a man in your life!'

The man in all their lives in those mid-thirties years was that blond and golden boy Edward, Prince of Wales — until he took up with 'that Simpson one' and let her carry him off like the Widow Quinn in *The Playboy* against the gorgeous girls of the western world! Our sister dropped him like a hot potato then — having first driven Mother crazy by insisting that we get

41

the wireless for his coronation — and she fell in instead with a line of film stars: Valentino of course and Douglas Fairbanks, Errol Flynn, Franchot Tone and Gary Cooper; Clark Gable, who played Blackie in *San Francisco* to Spencer Tracy's Father Flanagan — a priest and a celibate but, like those Dominicans on Pope's Quay, remarkably handsome and all-male! And of course Leslie Howard, who had a face and a head like a Nordic god; every time a film of *his* came on, the whole gaggle trooped off in style to see it. When they came back, they would lock themselves in 'the room', the sewing-machine would be put to one side but the teapot would not, and all night there would be fresh brewings, all aimed at the crucial fortune sought by each and heard in deadly silence, of a tall blond man about to enter their lives!

It could hardly last. A relative came home on holiday from Dagenham and lured her back with her — the promise of a job with real money was too much to turn down. 'Sure, won't you be back home for Christmas?' the cousin plied, 'think of the style you'll have to show off then!'

There was a party in the house the night before she left, and the fortune-telling/dressmaking friends all came in. When it was over and they had gone, a neighbour-woman came to collect the sewing-machine, which she had bought. Up to that, the reality of her going had not struck us; but the sight of it going out the door brought us alive — it was like someone's coffin being carried away. Mother started, then we were all at it. I fled upstairs and hid my head under a pillow where no-one would see me. I don't think any of us realised till then how much we loved her.

Our grief was short-lived. Within a year she was back — Hitler had the sirens wailing over London, but I like to think she came more because she missed us too than for the death and danger of life over there. The sewing-machine came back with her — that was her year's saving gone! — and with it came the girls and women once more, the dressmaking and the fortunes, and the whole whirligig of the Streetsinger and Alice Benbolt started up again — not forgetting Leslie Howard, who was about to burst upon the scene in a new marvel of blond incorruptibility as Ashley Wilkes in David O. Selznick's *Gone With The Wind*.

It is not the end of the story, but it is near enough the end to be nearly able to finish it here. Not quite though. Within another year, she had married and gone from us for good. It wasn't Clark Gable nor Gary Cooper, and sure as hell it wasn't Leslie Howard, Father, Son and Holy Ghost to them all! But he was a good man, and they had a good life together for a few years. We kept in touch with her, we came to see her and she came to us, and the same brightness was always about her — but I leave all that now to be remembered or forgotten like the flotsam and jetsam of all our lives, and jump ahead to the next time I hid from people to avoid being seen in a state about her.

This was a dozen years on when the injured leg did what it had always been threatening to do: it became incurably tuber-culous, the disease spread like a fast tide through her, and the poultices and prayers to Our Lady of Lourdes were no use to her any more. By then I had gone from home, but the crippled girl who had held me against my infant incubus was still there some-where in the background and in a few scrawled lines she told me of an incubus of her own:

> The family are all well including Daddy except myself who am poorly this time. The time is long when you're in bed especially the likes of me could never take it. Sometimes I think I'm dying, the nuns start saying rosaries and things, I'm sure there'd be a big black tea-leaf on the lip of my cup if someone could read it. But I'm getting up for Easter when you come down and we'll have a few songs and the girls will come and it'll be like old times ...

I did come down, but it wasn't she who was there but some changeling in the bed in her place. Her face was gone, there was nothing but the big blue eyes fighting the grief she saw in mine. When I left her, I fled into the clean air where there was no God only the God of the living, of those of us who must live after seeing such things and try to forget. But the memory of her standing between chairs, holding herself erect while she danced the hornpipe on uneven legs, of the tea-leaves and the cups and the chatter about fortunes — it was all there as it had never before been there, because it would never again be there now.

Her great pal Madgie Murphy led the troupe of pals as they walked beside the coffin. She'd have liked them that night, bright to the last, rouge and lipstick and high stiletto heels! Blaise Pascal's God, 'more exigent than the theologians', can relax his rules for them: their time was a time for a little laughter — thereafter, Death, where was thy sting?

We buried her in Douglas with our father, his first and dearest child. Our mother and eldest brother are now there too — the four of them once more together, as they had been before we all came along. Pray for them if you have a mind. They would not reject it.

5

SWEET SINGING IN THE CHOIR

READING OVER what I have written, it may seem that I am writing a sad book. I suppose in some ways I am. But there was also the other side. For one thing, our house was always full of singing. To this day I have dozens of songs by heart, all learnt at home or picked up line by scrapy line on that old His Master's Voice of my sister's. Anyone who could harmonise was especially welcome, which in turn led to an even more passionate involvement; the very sound was enough, without words at all, to get the crowd in.

The words as often as not were made up as we went along — any sort of words, sense or nonsense, as long as they filled the lines. So the story of the fat woman in the rowing boat shouting at her husband, 'Sing, Henry, like the gondolas do!' made more sense to us than to many for, if gondolas could sing, then by all means let them. Everyone else did — including the gondoliers, if *they* had a mind! Local prowess was not infrequently measured by how well one could lead a crowd in a chorus at a party or in a pub, though our singing happened in all sorts of other places as well.

In all that wide and varied family circle, I can remember only one member who never sang. That was my Uncle Timmy, a stolid man with bluebell eyes and a pipe clenched between granite jaws. The secret of his silence may have lain in an experience he had had while lying shell-shocked in the mud of No Man's Land. The dead and dying were about him everywhere, and as the German scouting patrol went past, bayoneting anyone who still showed signs of life, he realised that his sole chance of survival was to look deader than anyone else. This required such a feat of concentration that it burnt a frozen pose upon him for the rest of his life. Later he was picked up and taken prisoner, locked up with his pipe and his silences for the full duration, and then sent back home, safe and sound with a pension which, though small, was yet big enough to keep him in single comfort for the rest of his life.

The pension was bigger than Father's — a disparity that rankled with someone who had endured the full burden of the war. Though brothers, you really would wonder how two such totally different people could come out of the same house. This difference would come to a head on Christmas nights when Mother, always a great one for family loyalty, would insist that Father go over and bring his only brother back. He would grumble a bit but eventually go and, either from boredom or loneliness on the Holy Night, some remote chord of affection would be touched in Timmy by the sight of his mercurial brother coming to him on so solemn an occasion. Not alone would he always come, but he would be moved miraculously to speech. But as ill-luck would have it, his speech turned upon the one subject only — misfortune, what else but Father's war! To make matters worse, he talked at such a pace that, not to mind his own one but the Hundred Years War itself would be over by the time he had done. 'We were in Fra-a-a-nce ... it was the dead of night ... I was on sentry go-o-o ... ' We had heard it all many times before, the same story, the same voice — we'd all be asleep by the time he was half-way there: all except Father, who got steadily crosser and more restive as the drone went on. Mother would do her best to try to edge him on, she'd be pushing fresh bottles of stout between them to quicken the pace — but it didn't work, Father's fuse was burning too fast.

Then, finally, he'd blow. 'What-in-the-name-of-Christ war are you talking about? What war did you ever see, that got your-self locked up safe and sound for three years and nine months and left poor eejits like us to do the fighting!' In one of the rare rapid movements of his life, Timmy would have his cap and be up and away. Mother would start to bawl: for Jesus, Mary and Joseph's sake, would he sit down and not be making a show of her before the children, leaving her house on the holy and blessed Christmas Night! Father didn't mean it, he had a few drinks taken, they'd all be better in the morning!

That was the final stroke, and drove him wild altogether. There was only one way now of heading off the disaster — that was by singing. To this, even the offended prisoner-of-war could

46

not but give assent; from the loneliness of his own little place, I suppose ours must have seemed like a heaven. The olive branch was put out and taken, and soon the prince of peace was back in our midst again. What a fine contrast to all that were some of the songs we then sang:

> Oh, of all places the wild world around,
> Home is the best, dearest home.
> Happier spot have our feet never found,
> Home is the best, dearest home.
> Father and Mother make holy the place,
> Sisters and brothers adorn it with grace,
> Gentle affection illumines each face,
> Home is the best, dearest home!

The fact that everyone sang meant that we were never without willing volunteers; it also meant that we had to listen to the most awful bores. Billy Callanan, an undertaker's mute with a professionally sad face, had to be let go through the whole ten verses of *Ten Green Bottles Hanging on the Wall;* while Billy Lynch, my brother's driver, raced through his songs without pretending to sing them at all, the words coming out in short spurts like machine-gun fire, which ceased when his face, gone puce from 'singing', turned its normal colour again. Paul Robeson was every bass's dream, and when Dave Leahy sang *In Cellar Cool I Sit at Ease* his voice died to an asthmatic wheeze long before he got half way down the octave 'D-r-i-n-k-i-n-g'! Another cousin, Johnny Buckley, took such a shine to the 'Streetsinger,' that he sang *My Mother's Birthday Today* with all the r's and a's gone:

> It's my muddaw's bockdee to-dee,
> I'm on my wee with a lovely bouquee,
> And I know what that means to comvee,
> For tis my muddaw's bockdee to-dee!

All this singing came to a head in the church choir, which was the one place where some semblance of order prevailed. In this way church and pub played in fairly close association, though neither would ever admit it. So when Jimmy Coyle shot the high wire in church on Sunday mornings with his marvellous searing tenor — 'Jer-ey-rus-al-em, Jey-ey-rus-al-eh-em!' — the other male voices who had been with him in 'The Mountain' the night

47

before intercepted his rocket in mid-flight and brought him safely down to earth in fine bass-baritone convoy. The 'Mountain' version was, of course the secular *Jerusalem (The Holy City)* as sung by Richard Crooks, the American tenor who sang out of a wheelchair; signs on it, half the tenors in Cork were out of their minds trying to get into wheelchairs to be able to sing like him! Father McCarthy, the choirmaster, had enough sense to know that 'The Mountain' was as good as any organ-loft to dry-test his singers, and he gave it the blind eye as he passed it on Saturday night and heard his larks in the clear air striking notes he hoped wouldn't be choked from the fog of cigarette smoke by the time he got them the following morning.

Another conductor, a Bavarian, Aloys Fleischmann, came as a refugee and stayed to make a determined effort at turning the barefoot urchins around the Cathedral into the Vienna Boys Choir; Gerard Brady of the Dominicans, aloof and exacting and a perfectionist, knew what an organ could do to make even a poor choir good; and in tow with him was the choirmaster, Harry Whitehouse, fat and excitable and stammering like a steam engine — until he sang, when what came out was such a golden glory that you'd wonder to God why he bothered with a choir at all and didn't do the singing himself!

Drink was central to all this, with one notable exception: our Uncle Jimmy, Mother's youngest brother, who did not drink at all. As a younger man he had given up a good job in Ryan's soap factory, the vapours from the melting tallow being thought harmful to delicate lungs. But he went on to be a mighty eighty-five, the last quarter century of which he did by being the heart and centre of our whole singing tribe. Everyone wanted him, he always came; he was often the only sober man there. He was also blessed with an uncanny ability to rise wave by wave with the alcohol level and eventually out-top them all. Often, when we were younger, he would come over to the house and sing in harmony with us the songs we had learnt at school; I remember his beautiful mellow voice turning my reedy soprano to a lovely rich sound in the harmony section of the Brahms Lullaby in Irish — neither of us having the smallest idea what the words meant:

> Soondereeha iss law, iss na hangill i draw,
> Soondereeha iss law, is na hah-in-gill i draw.

48

What we were singing were the perfectly sensible words in Irish:

Suaimhneas oíche is lá,
Is na haingil i dtráth

which freely translates into something like:

Tranquil night-time and noon,
And the angels in tune.

This Jimmy must have learnt somewhere the secret of phrasing, because he could make perfectly simple songs we all knew well sound completely different. Moore's Melodies were great favourites, especially *Oft in the Stilly Night*, which he would sing with our younger sister to restore the family peace on one of those shaky Christmas Nights. Maybe it was his native sobriety or maybe some basic hardness unknown to the rest of us, but he was also the only man who could shake us out of the Jesus-weeps with which the family seemed to be cursed when the tearjerker sessions began.

Father could never get through *Michael Dwyer* without crying, and when his big crying verse came on — the one in which 'up stood the brave MacAllister, the weak and wounded man' to give his life for his comrades — Father would start to blubber, and the whole house would be in a knot trying to get him through it — which of course only made him twice as determined to carry on. That was the sad end of many a night, but for Uncle Jimmy with one of his rabble-rousing choruses: *Phil the Fluther's Ball, Tread on the Tail of Me Coat* (in the course of which he'd stand out in the middle of the floor and throw off his own coat as if to threaten all us Murphys when he came to the line: 'I licked all the Murphys afloat!'), or *The Bould Thady Quill*, a full-throated ballad about Cork's holy trinity of hurling, drinking and politics.

As he got older, his songs got better; he seemed to put more meaning into them, and his lovely plangent voice would lie upon the notes, reminding you that he had feeling all right, even though he often tried to hide it — as he did the night he came over to the house to tell us that his mother, our grandmother, had died, the tears running all over his lined and craggy face and dropping like raindrops from the point of his chin. Strangely, he never shed a tear at all that any of us could see when his own wife

49

died, leaving him with all the children still to rear — though you'd hear the break in his voice sometimes, years later, when he sang a song like *Absence:*

> Then may the good God guide you on your way,
> Guard and protect your footsteps lest they stray,
> Until we meet on God's eternal shore,
> Never to part, dear, never to part no more.

But that was all over and done with now; the children *were* reared, and Jimmy, now an old but still incredibly vibrant man, became the centre of our whole singing tribe. We brought him everywhere with us: to weddings and christenings, to hurling and football matches, to every event both in grief and celebration; and a whole new generation of singers grew up around him and got to know when he was around. A world grown up on 'flower power' and anti-nuclear songs, to say nothing of Bob Dylan's 'Universal Soldier', had no time for Wallace's *Let me like a Soldier Fall*, though he would still sing it for one of the oldies if they asked:

> Let me only think of that proud race
> Which ends its blaze with me,
> To die the last but not disgraced,
> An ancient chivalry.
> Though o'er my grave no banners wave
> Nor trumpets requient swell,
> Howe'er forgot unknown my tomb,
> I like a soldier fell!
> Howe'er forgot unknown my tomb,
> I like a soldier fell!

But if they didn't want that, and they didn't, he learnt their own songs — and sang them better, more sweetly and with more conviction that any of them did: like the Beach Boys' *Sloop John B,* which he turned into one of the new national anthems at the Munster hurling finals, with a whole new generation of throatful choristers behind him, none of them seeing the living irony in the old man's words:

> We sailed on the sloop *John B,*
> My gran'pappy and me,
> All over the seven seas we did roam.

Went drinking all night,
Got into a fight;
I feel so broke up, I wanna go home!

His last outing, appropriately enough, was to a wedding: it was one of his grand-nephews, my brother's son, Timmy Murphy, who had won the honours in the beloved red and white jersey of Cork. It had been close on seventy years since the old man had pulled on a jersey himself. There is a photograph of him from that time; the little boy out front as mascot is our eldest brother, the young groom's father — by now, like most of the rest of them, dead. He was, as always, insuppressible: old songs for the old, new songs for the young — but young and old all came together in a last hurrah for what had then become known to us as his very own stamp and signature tune: and I write it here not in sorrow or in sadness but in jubilation for a tribe who sang for love and who loved to sing, and whose ha'p'orth of songs made us masters for a little of a brief not inglorious day:

Those were the days, my friends,
We thought they'd never end,
We'd sing and dance forever and a day;
We'd live the life we choose,
We'd fight and never lose,
Those were the days, my friends, those were the days.

6

WILD VALERIAN

ALL THE singing, however, was but a break from a grind so hopeless and without future that, if one were conscious of it, it could — in some cases did — drive people mad. In this way, our singing parties were a wild fling at a satisfaction we would never have in real life at all. We sang to escape life, not confront it. There was only one way that could be done, and that was through education.

The vast majority did not see it that way, and went to school with no fixed purpose other than to fulfil the statutory obligation. The SAO — school attendance officer — was a dreaded figure in the street; instinctively we caught the nicety of the legal position in that parent and child were equally in trouble if he called. It was nothing at all to see a mother literally drag her child to school in the mornings, the recalcitrant clinging to the railings in wild and anguished protest; then, to compound his terror, the Brother standing at the gate, strap barely concealed beneath the cassock, to greet his unwilling scholar.

Most pupils left as soon as they could, going on to small jobs as messenger boys or hod-carriers, workers in factories or, if they were lucky, apprentices to their fathers' trades.

Great numbers emigrated. Our ship, the *Innisfallen,* was green and white, and sailed like a haughty conquistador down the river past the rusty hulks stuck in the mud, bearing the best of our young friends away. For those who stayed, the object was to earn enough to be able to afford a packet of Woodbines or go to the pictures, a blind and terminal life succoured by such small benefits. One could not blame the parents for this, the only difference between the generations being that they in their time had done the same, only for less, and younger.

Father had left school finally at the age of eight; Mother never spoke about school at all. Years later, when she had to sign the cheque that brought me my scholarship money, the 'X, her mark' shamed me so much that I laboured through many hours trying to teach her to write her name. She could manage the 'Julia' well enough; that extraordinary feat of association between the trailing spider-line and her name seemed to have registered from an earlier time; but the surname was quite beyond her. 'Bad luck to my schoolmistress!' was her valediction to a time when the miracle of writing might have been achieved but was not; so the 'X, her mark' remained and I burned with shame, standing in the queue beside her while some malevolent clerk forced the admission from her for all the world to hear.

This was no different from other families in the street; in fact, we were unusual in that we were among the few who bothered with secondary school at all. It is difficult to say exactly where this educational thrust came from, though clearly our unschooled but intelligent father must during his army days have gained some notion of what education could do; and our muddled but steadfast mother picked this up in a way that made the triple leap from hope through work to the rewards of a steady job. There was also the good fortune of the attendant times: a country newly won to independence, with new prospects opening up; a whole new world where the educated boy or girl could win a place among the privileged ones of the earth.

One has to mention here the marvellous Christian Brothers, philanthropic educators of the emergent poor. They took vows of poverty, chastity, and obedience — the most important of which, from our point of view, was poverty, because it meant they could teach us for nothing! They carried about with them a trinity of virtues: godliness, national fervour, and a kind of scrubbed and Calvinistic discipline that was wholly approved of as an essential for advancement to the good life.

If a boy bucked the Brothers, he was in for a rough time; parents acquiesced in this, hoping that school discipline alone would do the trick, but even then one could see that the vital ingredient would be one's personal work, that it would take time and effort on one's own part — with the places so few, inevitably the drop-out rate would be high. 'Why should he be wastin' his time with old books in that place when he could be out earnin'?' was a stock parental response to the suggestion that a bright boy might go on to secondary school. University was undreamt of:

learning for its own sake would have been a meaningless blasphemy, the sole credible target for the acquisition of book-knowledge being the examination, which was the stepping-stone to a better, that is to say a white-collar, life.

There was a time when I might have avoided it all: I was a milkman's boy and happy at it, and might have gone quite another way. It was a job most of us youngsters living on the fringes of the town could pick up easily, the roundsmen coming in with their full churns each morning, glad of the help to get the milk to the customers before they got up. You met your rounds-man early, seven or seven-thirty, then ran the round with your two-gallon can and pint measure till it was time to go to school. In summer, there were two deliveries a day, so you met again when school was over and spent the rest of the day doing the second half of the round. For that, at the end of the week, you got the princely sum of sixpence — a 'tanner' we called it — but that wasn't all: a milkman's boy was soon left to tackle and untackle the horse; sometimes you were even given the reins, a rare thrill with a strong young horse, adding further to a rich and absorbing life in which there was no sense other than the sense of being alive, with neither future nor past nor anything at all but the enveloping present to hold you.

The farm was five miles from town; it had a cobbled yard and when you drove the horse and van across the cobbles at mid-day, it made a grand rollicking sound as if to say how glad they were to see us back. My job then was to unyoke the sweating cob and lead him to the stables where there was a great smell of dung and hay; in winter, plumes of white fanned out from the nostrils of the other horses as they champed and trampled on the trodden straw. On Sundays, we played hurling with the hired hands in the fields and, when we came in burning hot from the game, the place to go was the dairy, a plain stone room, cold as a tomb and with no light but the light from the whitewashed walls and the gleaming steel of the churns standing about. If you were thirsty then, you could dip a cup in the churn and slowly swallow the icy cream, smooth as ivory, and bliss to a twelve-year-old animal boy.

If I came home late on Sunday nights, the homework I had not done and did not want to do was there like a leaden load before me; I saw and wanted nothing then but to be back on my farm, a milkman's oaf on sixpence a week, with the long-term ambition that one day I might become a milkman myself, with my own horse and my very own milk-round.

That was in a time before I was born, my world a world of animals and farmyards, of the reek of horses and the swish of milk in the pails at milking time, and the sudsy white liquid plashing all day long into my two-gallon can; my greatest ambition, if I had one, to be able to tackle and untackle a horse faster than anyone else. Could I have stayed so? Could I have gone on and grown up to be that man? Was there another me inside the me I became, someone who got lost somewhere on the way, never to be heard of again? I doubt it. Is there any life but the life one lives, any choice but the choice one makes? All I know is that that was a time that was as real as anything that is now real, and I was a me as real as the me I now am — and both were strangers to the time that now is. With wonder and amazement I ask myself, what miracle of events brought such changes about? For all that had stopped suddenly one day, and I had gone another way.

As I trudged across the city from our new Corporation house on the south side to the old Blarney Street Christian Brothers' school on the north which, as a point of honour, I could not leave since my brothers before me had gone there, all along the Rock Steps on the way up to the school, wild valerian grew out from the walls, its white and pink and crimson blooms hectic and beautiful — and utterly ignored in our blind and abject lives.

The Brothers knew Mother well and recognised in her the true object of their vocational zeal: the poor but dauntless Irish mother struggling against debt and damnation to bring her numerous brood to a better and easier life. There is a sense in which she actually loved them, a love three parts gratitude for their altruistic service and one regret that she so desperately needed it. To her dying day, she would go into raptures at the mere mention of their name and when, later in life, she developed a most unlikely passion for the game of hurling, it was nothing to do with the game at all, but rather that it was the game at which the Christian Brothers' boys excelled — including a recent Taoiseach, Jack Lynch, whom she knew and loved as she loved her own sons.

There were no fees at primary level, a mere pittance of a few pounds at secondary; if there was real need, the Brothers would not demand even that. Even more, they would covertly see to it that the boys in really desperate circumstances were actually clothed and fed; sometimes the lay teachers did this too. Extra-curricular grinds were there for the asking: it wasn't the Brothers but the boys who couldn't be got to come. Such grinds were for scholarships, and by the end of my primary school days it had begun to dawn on me that I might just about get one.

A new principal had come to the school; he had the name of being a truly terrible man. Small, bald and fat, with the sensuous lips of a lover who had never known love, he came to us with the brand of the destroying angel to scourge our small lives with taunt, belittlement and withering derision; this, backed by the power of terrifying rages, soon made him a nightmare in the school. As I crossed the city each morning to the acrid smell of hops brewing in the vats of Beamish's, its reek became synonymous with dread of another day of black misanthropy. Boys literally fled from the place when he came at them: Paddy Foran, an agile youth tall beyond his years, got through a window in the nick of time and was never seen in school again; Willie John Cooney, seeing him beat his younger brother, went for him from behind and made for the door, the young brother with him, before the angel of vengeance could catch them up. But his aim was clear: to create a name for his slum school and make scholars of at least a few of its half-starved, barefoot urchins. Alas, there being only ten places, he had but a slim chance; but it was that chance, once achieved, that would make one's name for good.

So for the first time in my young life, I began to know the meaning of work. After school each day when the others had gone home, he would put in another two or three hours with the selected few. There we sat in the classroom dusk, a brave new world of post-colonial improvers, listening to the blackbirds in the monks' orchard and, beyond, the cries of our young com-panions at play, while strange-sounding names like Wordsworth and Milton, Shelley and Keats, dived about us like swallows in the air.

Meanwhile, the more lurid aspects of the Brothers' discipline gained more notoriety: the 'strap' — in effect a short leather truncheon — could indeed be an instrument of savagery when wielded by a full-grown man; and I am certain that some boys' main recollection of their school-days is of that sad and evil instrument. But most of us, I think, understood what the basic motive was, and were either cunning or clever enough most of the time to avoid open confrontation. There were more ingenious forms of retribution: one Brother, much revered by the parents, liked to punish his errants by lifting them bodily by the sidelocks off the ground; another practised aiming his strap sideways onto the fingertips — making, if one could spare a thought for it, a nice popping sound like a plucked string as it swished past the wrongdoer's fingers. It was normal for such teachers to be hated and feared, and when it got to breaking point the boy would make a run for it, shouting as he went that he'd 'get his father down!' When the father came — or, what was worse, the big brother — there was a delicious moment of imminent revenge as the whole school waited for the thunder of the avenger's boots on the rough boards. 'Come out, ye bastard, and meet your match!' would notify all and sundry that the moment had come. Some brothers — Tipperary-men, I seem to remember, were notably brave — would take this in their stride and, since it was a sacrilege to hit a priest or Brother in his cloth, would take the challenge head-on by pulling off the dog-collar as they went to meet the prospective assailant. The scandal of such confrontation could not be tolerated, and the Head Brother would usually get there first to draw the danger off.

Such teachers, however, did not get good results: even at that early stage in the dark ages of education, what worked best was the teacher who could get on with his class without intimidation; where that was there, the inept and foolish resort to punishment and retribution could be wholly dispensed with.

One day, in a history class, such a teacher brought in some pieces from the local museum where he was doing research work. 'Just think,' he said as he handed them around, 'that boys of your age held those very axe-heads in their hands and used them for splitting firewood maybe thousands of years ago!' The thought lodged in one's mind and lit up a whole new world, the long unbroken line from father to son since civilisation in Ireland began! History with that teacher was a dream and we loved it.

But, with or without it, there was now this strange new urge to work and to win, a heady mixture even at so young an age, needing no other stimulation. The object was not aesthetic or cultural or anything like that — quite simply to get that scholarship and be able to pay one's way through the next phase, which with luck and labour might yet end up in the dreamed-of white-collar job in the civil service. So when spring came that year and the wild valerian began to burst into bloom on the Rock Steps, it brought with it tidings of new hope and new horizons in a new and growing world. We sat our scholarship examination at Easter and, like the 'course' athletes we now were, we gave it all we had: all the soaked-up knowledge of the previous months, the facts and figures, the data, dates and dimensions, the words and grammar, structures and similes, syntax, sums and surds — it all came out now in a dozen crammed hours that would determine the course of our future lives. It was a race, and we ran to win. And, while we ran, we prayed to God for luck and fortune to fill the gaps where we ourselves were lacking.

That was Easter; by the following August I had forgotten those early spring days. Then one Friday coming up towards the end of the month there was a flurry in the street and someone came banging at the door. Mother opened it; it was a neighbour-boy, all flushed and out of breath, having run from the Corporation office in the City Hall, where a clerk had told him that 'a William Murphy from beside where you live has got first place in the city scholarship!'

I went down to enquire and found it was true. By the time I got back, the house was in an uproar; my invalid sister, now married, had taken her infant son from the cot where he had started to wail from the unaccustomed cheering and was lulling him back to sleep — and praying to God that some day, some place, the same honour and glory would come to him! Such, such were the dreams of our ha'penny world, and such the pinnacles of our penny-ha'penny fame!

It was a good feeling; all the work was now worth while. But, over and above the feeling, there was a sense of confidence that, having done it once, one could do such things again. I did not know it then, but from that moment the course of my future life was settled.

7

GOODBYE, LITTLE YELLOW BIRD!

Goodbye, little bird, I'd rather brave the cold
In a world that's free than a prisoner be
In a cage of gold!
> — Music-hall song from the
> film of Oscar Wilde's *The Picture of Dorian Gray.*

THE LOCAL boy made good has all the ingredients of the fable: life owes him nothing, gives nothing he does not win; but winning itself is motivation — there is only one way to go when that far down, and that is up. So even little steps become big ones, and even a thimbleful of glory every bit as full as the great-sounding casks of the world.

From now on school was always less work than play: competitive play, play to win with all one's strength and wits, but still play. The game itself was fun once you had learnt to look at it that way. Mastery of the skills was like being able to cycle or swim or do anything else at all well. All sorts of faculties came into it: memory, invention, ingenuity, stamina, imagination — even the occasional flash of inspiration, which could happen even at that age and was well above the ordinary pursuit of excellence. The American Robert Penn Warren puts it well: 'It is my experience that the dream comes to the man who has done the work.'

No effort was too great, no detail too slight, no midnight oil too late to waste on the desired achievement.

I was well into secondary school in the North Monastery now, the Leaving Cert was the target; but it was 1946, the war was over, and the civil service and the semi-states were beginning to open up and recruit people again. So one went hell-bent for them. One learnt by heart long poems like *Paradise Lost* or the

Irish saga *Agallamh Oisín agus Pádraig*, and thought nothing of the labour in it. Later on, like everyone else, I became sceptical about this — until I heard Auden say on radio one night that he attributed much of his literary success to the fact that as a boy he had been forced to learn thousands of lines of verse by heart! For us, such fine questions of pedagogy did not arise: there was work to be done, we had learnt how to do it, we would now continue with purpose towards the treasured prize. We needed those scholarships, not for educational purposes only but to help buttress family finances — to the point where, for instance, they made the difference between a full and a meagre table on Christmas Day. So we rejoiced in our one-star luck that brought us such bonanzas to see us through the enveloping, but now dissolving, dark. But sooner or later the schooling would cease and one would have to get a job. In some ways, I would have been better off at university, where I later got scholarships too and actually went for a while as an arts student.

Amongst my teachers in University College Cork was Harry Atkins, Professor of Mathematics and a truly sophisticated man. Fresh from Leaving Certificate where we counted our A's as Red Indians counted scalps, to us he was, I'm afraid, very much a voice in the wilderness as he retaught us the simple process of the unitary method that we had learnt in primary school — but now we were invited to look at it not for the answer but for 'the beauty of the concept'. The very words were strange. A beauty furthermore, he said, that was indefinable except to the sophisticated mind that could contemplate its beauty, savour it, as one savoured a Beethoven sonata or the taste of strawberries and cream! This was a different approach from the Christian Brothers (where, however, I was happy to note, Professor Atkins had had his early education too!) Bill Porter, a classics scholar, discoursed on the bucolic delights of Horace and left in the evenings on an old rusty bicycle to return to his Sabine farm in Douglas where, we were told, he would occasionally notice one of his beautiful children and enquire earnestly how was its father! Professor Treston was a sterner sort: he looked like Wagner and had the same weighty tones; Virgil was his great strength, and at night he foregathered with old friends in the snug of Henchy's at Dillon's Cross to discourse on the familial pieties of '*pius Aeneas*': pieties, one felt, that made up for the reported loss of religion in the learned man's own life, though it was also reported that he had a brother a bishop in Africa — a fact which he couldn't seem to make up his mind whether he wanted to remember or forget!

The Irish teachers were an undistinguished lot, with the exception of Cormac Ó Cuilleanáin, who seemed to me to personify the beauty of the Munster oral tradition. His wife, Eilís Dillon, whom I did not know then, was the author of some fine children's books and later on a fine novel, *Across the Bitter Sea*; and his daughter Eilean, a generation on, would become one of the best young poets and scholars of her time. In the English Department a haughty lady by the name of B. G. McCarthy lectured on Chaucer to classes which, for the most part, were not far advanced beyond what they might have been in Chaucer's time; but she did give glimpses of the Franciscan innocence of those extraordinary tales.

Dominating the whole scene, in fact in many ways the only abiding influence that that college would have in the first century of its life, was the limping, bespectacled figure of Daniel Corkery, Professor of English — and a man who had never been to university himself at all. Corkery had written plays and several books of short stories — *A Munster Twilight, Earth Out of Earth, The Hounds of Banba* — and one beautiful and evocative novel, *The Threshold of Quiet*. This resembled Turgeney's work, of which he was a great admirer; also Alain Fournier's *Les Grandes Meaulnes* (translated as *The Milk of Paradise*), which had the same crystalline purity, tinged with horror and grief. Those stories and the novel had been written long before; under the influence of the Gaelic League, perhaps especially his close friend Terence MacSwiney, Corkery had become, with Douglas Hyde and Eoin MacNeill, one of the main apologists for cultural renewal through the Irish language; and his major works, *The Hidden Ireland* and *Synge and Anglo-Irish Literature*, are text-books in universities to this day.

At that time I was too fresh to university life to be able to appreciate him or to make any but the most cursory and superficial use of the wealth and riches of his extraordinary visionary mind; but I was lucky to have met him and to have laid the foundations for what were many pleasant and stimulating hours spent in his company later on in the little bungalow looking out over Cork harbour, long after I had left Cork and university behind.

But, inherited wisdom said that a bright boy was 'wastin' his time with books in that oul' place when he could be out earnin'', and leave university I did, in January 1947 at the very first opportunity. This was when I got a job in the civil service — that of clerical officer, ambition of all local boys in those years — and off I went to Dublin.

The office was in the Lower Castle Yard, gaunt brick fronts and hideous rooms despite the glad new colours of the Board of Works, with creaking staircases and windows that rattled like old ghosts when the lorries went down Ship Street, heartland of Dublin argot, which I was to hear there for the very first time.

From the start it was a fiasco: all the years of study and schooling were suddenly dumped aside while one was set the most repetitive and mechanical tasks, which could just as easily have been done by a child. Scarcely knowing the word, and having no insight into its fundamental importance in the national life, I was assigned to the Statistics Office, and set to work on the national cost of living figure.

My boss, a timid little man by the name of Tim Kiely, smiled ceaselessly in ingratiation like a piece of cold fish between bread slices. He moaned piteously about 'the bloody cost o' livin'' and I, with my Cork background still close to me, sympathised with him — until I realised that he wasn't talking about the cost of living at all, but about some statistical description of it, about which I couldn't at the time have cared less! Such concepts do not enter young people's minds. He lived in daily terror of *his* bosses who were in adjoining rooms and were, he said, always on the prowl to catch and devour him. The lord and master of us all, an old-time civil servant by the name of Stanley Lyon, sat on a plush chair on a dais, and sometimes put him into coronary confusion when he summoned him to his presence.

The girls on the staff alternately bullied and flirted with him and left him powerless to control them, which of course had its nemesis when he had to face the music if the job wasn't done. Tea was constantly being brewed in dark corners to keep melancholy away, and covert little groups met in special rooms like secret societies, each member's cracked cup being his or her insignia and admission card to the club. Meanwhile, we kept an ear to the slamming of the glass door down the corridor and the footfall on the trembling boards of Donny Horgan, the Senior Staff, a truly terrifying man with all the might and rigours of his august rank. The 'temps' — temporary clerical assistants, lowest of the low and dismissible at a week's notice — lived in daily dread of him: one wrong move and they were out. A smile from him was money in the bank; a frown, nights of sleepless anxiety.

If ever there was a place where unions were needed, it was in that sad little scene of discreet and craven servitude. Signs on it, there was always someone going out sick with ulcers, nervous exhaustion, or other forms of psychosomatic debility. I did my best with it, knowing that at the very first chance I would get out. A lot of others there had the same idea: Pádraig Ó hUigín, a studious and perceptive man, went on to become an international local government and housing expert and is now secretary of the Department of the Taoiseach; Con Collins and Austin Kennan went on to equally successful careers; Dónal Nevin, who was a great favourite with the girls, went into the trade union movement and is now general secretary of the Irish Congress of Trade Unions; while Gerard Victory, whose head was full of notes when it should have been full of figures, threw statistics aside on his marriage day and went on to a highly successful career in the only field he really cared about, ending up as RTE's respected Director of Music. Of the older men, Gabriel Fallon, friend of Seán O'Casey and one of the leading lights of the early Abbey Theatre, had come to terms with the place, and in any case lived his real life elsewhere; and Roy Geary, who was indeed a statistician of worth, had such a burning passion for the national well-being that he was probably the only one there who could have fired us with his enthusiasm, if only he could have got near us at all.

All of this became evident to me later; but for now my sole concern was to get out. The next grade above me was that of executive officer, the ultimate aim of all bright boys in those years. It was got by open competition, so the whole process started up again: the books and targets, the timetables and study-plans and midnight oil — only this time, locked up with my Gogol mates all day, frozen to death in unheated digs all night, it was a time for a rugged sense of purpose and a strong and fervent will. I don't know which came first, disillusionment with what I was doing all day or the hope of ending it which made me work all night, but in any case I did get the result I wanted — with a vengeance too. I was placed first yet again, and so my time in Statistics was at an end. The Senior Staff came crashing through the glass door; I could hear his marauding hooves thundering up the corridor. Let him be the first to congratulate me; he had always known I was a bright boy! Yes, he would prophesy right now I would go far! Well, I was out now, I didn't have to worry about him!

I felt a little pang of sadness leaving the 'temps' though; especially poor timid little Molly Moss, who loved her own Dublin poor so much that she couldn't bear the thought of becoming one of them! Through all that time they were gentle and concerned people who made what could have been a most unpleasant time enjoyable. They reminded me of T. S. Eliot's phrase about Mary Magdalene: 'the unoffending feet'. Now that I was leaving, I knew I would miss them.

So here I was, in the last year of my teens, having reached the pinnacle of all local boys of those years, first in the executive officers. If I had been told in the days of the wild valerian that my muddled and disjointed efforts would have come to this, I would not have believed it. It was mid-December when the news broke and, like all the others gone to glory in Dublin civil servitude, I went back down home to Cork for Christmas. The news was still fresh by the time I got down; there had been a photograph in the *Examiner*; when the train came in there were the old pals waving the school flag and cheering as if we had won a match.

Was it any more than that? Was there anything else apart from the immediate flush of victory? There had to be; I couldn't have come all this way for nothing. The midnight oil and the study, the memorising and work, all the cramming, target-setting and target-getting, all the times when one could have been out enjoying oneself when, instead, one stuck one's head in dusty books and kept it there till the subject was grasped and mastered — it couldn't all evaporate now into some dull, anonymous job! It would have to be something better, something singular and special. The fact that I was entering a service that employed several hundreds, if not thousands, of young people who all cherished the same hopes never seemed to occur to me. Having won my laurel wreath, *the* prize would have to be mine.

It is easy to see now that, with such an infantile build-up, I was riding for a fall. The fall came in the Department of Health, in the Custom House — I recall now that Richard Church, a writer whom I much admired, had had his fall in a custom house too: in London's, where he was stuck for all of twenty-six years! I was put to work on the administrative side of hospital construction — a good and exciting time to be there potentially, with the marvellous Dr Noël Browne of the ill-starred Mother and Child Scheme just about to come into control.

Browne was brilliant, patriotic, and deeply committed. He brought fire and zeal to a whole new attack upon the plague of tuberculosis, of which he had a burning personal and familial experience. He communicated to us all the same passionate and deeply held concern: hospitals and sanatoria sprang up overnight; wherever an old house or mansion could be adapted for use, it was bought at once and put into commission so as to isolate the disease-carriers and give some chance of recovery to those already infected as well as those at home. It was in its way a forerunner of that vibrant developmental scene that Seán Lemass had in mind ten years later with national development corporations such as Córas Tráchtála and the IDA. But I was too young, too totally ignorant of what the civil service was about to be able to make any sense of it.

From the very first I fell foul of its barren and futile officialdom, clogged up as it often is with unnecessary rules and regulations; I hated its rigid lines of demarcation and its vacuous sense of hierarchy. The dusty files took on a paranoic personality and the dry-and-dustier people gone to seed with them evoked at once my rage and my pity. Later, I wrote a story called 'The Anthill', which had one of these people going crazy from the ant-like concentration of building up his daily quota. The idea came from Gogol's *Diary of a Madman* — but the people were mine. It was a painful story to write: all that inertia and lack of verve bred by long habits of uninventiveness was there, the whole stupefying and blinkered rigor mortis of a life; in the story it comes out funny, but in life it was not. I felt robbed and cheated by it as if some vile pretence and deception had got me there in the first place. Nothing in my past had prepared me for it. The local boy had gone down his glory road, the laurel wreath about his neck; but the glory road turned out to be a glory hole, and the wreath a noose, and for more years then he now cares to remember, he became a very sad and unpromising morsel of humanity indeed.

It was this in a way that first led me to writing. I wrote because

I had to, it was the one real relief I had from the job. I suppose I hoped that sooner or later, though that might be very far away, it would eventually help me to get out. (I did not know then that it would, nor how.) Meanwhile what did help were the other equally tormented souls, roaming the corridors of other civil service offices and who, like me, were slaving away at the un-rewarding task in the hope that one day it might help them get free.

I wrote under the pen-name of Brian Fenton — the civil service didn't much approve of writers! The 'Brian' was from the first famous Kennedy — which was my father's christian name — Brian Ó Cinnéide, or Brian Bórú; while 'Fenton' was my grandmother's maiden name, on my mother's side.

Among the writers in the Custom House were some quite well-known names. Maurice Walsh, author of *Blackcock's Feather*, which I had loved as a boy, was an elegant and dsitinguished old man with a deerstalker hat and a caped coat like the one worn by Basil Rathbone in the old Sherlock Holmes films; Dónal Giltinan had written a rather touching if senti-mental Abbey success, *The Goldfish in the Sun*, set near Shandon in Cork; Pádraic Fallon wrote fine sinewy journalism and some imaginative verse; while the then Secretary of the Department of Local Government, John Garvin, was 'Andrew Cass', an expert on the writing of James Joyce. One of Garvin's principal officers in that department was Brian O'Nolan, who had written *At Swim Two Birds, The Dalkey Archive, An Béal Bocht* — a satire on the more preposterous side of the Irish revival movement — and later wrote savagely witty journalism in the columns of the *Irish Times*.

From outposts afar came news of other lost souls: Jack Keyes Byrne (Hugh Leonard), then a 'temp' in the Land Commission but already launched upon a career that would make him a brilliant theatre craftsman; and with him a company of lively and committed actors, notably Martin Dempsey, who later resigned to go acting full-time, Éamon Keane and Noel Ó Briain, who found refuge in Radio Éireann, and Mae Crowe and Tadhg Murray who stayed on to form the nucleus, with Séamus Páircéir (now Chairman of the Revenue Commissioners), of Gael-Linn's Halla Damer, the Irish-language theatre in Stephen's Green. The Land Commission group was called 'Lancos'; I have the feeling they got at least tacit encouragement from an influential and very senior Land Commissioner, Sam Waddell, who was himself a playwright and wrote under the rather portentous-sounding pseudonym 'Rutherford Mayne'. The 'Lancos' plays — including, if I am not mistaken, *The Italian Road*, and indeed all Hugh Leonard's early work — were done in the hall of the Royal Irish Academy of Music in Westland Row, where they had small audiences, a discouragement more than compensated for by the fact that they were most stylishly reviewed in the *Civil Service Review* (which was issued free and hence widely read) by Maurice Kennedy, husband of the novelist Val Mulkerns.

That kind of outpost of creative endeavour was a help to us all in our beleaguered plight. Another such outpost was the Department of External Affairs in Stephen's Green, from which one was constantly hearing of people like Máire Mhac an tSaoi, a scholarly woman and a poet; Conor Cruise O'Brien (now her husband), who wrote under the pseudonym 'Donat O'Donnell' and seemed to go on rather about Catholic writers; and a marvellously incisive drama critic, Thomas Hogan (again a pen-name: his real name was Thomas Woods, but following the pattern of anonymity, he didn't use it) who wrote, in Peadar O'Donnell's *Bell* and later John Ryan's *Envoy*, quite the most acerbic theatre notices I have ever seen.

But those were all successful writers, and I was far removed from that. Besides, apart from Hugh Leonard I don't think any of them had ever made it as clear as I had that they had no intention of staying in the job. That, in turn, brought its own retribution: if I didn't want it, then it didn't want me. So I found myself consigned to a company of amiable and rejected old codgers who had been passed over for the umpteenth time and were now steadily moving into the ranks of the chronic rejects.

One such was D. P. (David Patrick) Debrett, a big man with a face like Leo the Lion, who had come to accept his fate so totally that he renamed himself 'Don't Promote Debrett'! Once at an interview, when a questioner cast doubts upon the figure he gave for the acreage under wheat, he was reputed to have pulled a fiver out of his pocket, slapped it defiantly on the table and shot back: 'Cover that!' Another was J. L. Reilly, who had renamed himself 'Just Louse-Up Reilly'; he had been passed over so often, always unjustifiably in his view, that the injury to his pride turned him into a bitter but also rich man: scorning the job and wanting to show the people who had turned him down that he could make a life in spite of them, he set up a commercial school on the outskirts of Dublin that was so sought after that he could certainly have bought most of them out. But he stayed on, his poisoned scorn a living rebuke, or so he hoped, to the stupidity and vindictiveness of the petty men who could have helped him and did not. Promotion mattered hugely like that, not for the money so much as for a sense of self-esteem; in the peer group it was the mark of success, the interview board the vital life-hurdle.

As for me, I could not bring myself to be interested in it; not in interviews or promotion or anything else about it — hence I had to look elsewhere for a life.

I was turned twenty-one by now and beginning to feel that, if things didn't change soon, they never would. In a mood and at a time like that, you can do strange things. I wrote to Lord Dunsany, who long ago had adopted the poet Francis Ledwidge, and asked whether he mightn't do the same for another postulant now. A similar appeal went to the Earl of Wicklow — who, in those days, was head of the publishing house of Clonmore and Reynolds into which, though I had no knowledge of the trade, I felt I might have fitted quite well. Both, I felt, being rich, would be keen to help a struggling writer: that was two mistakes — I doubt if they were rich either! Certainly poor Billy Wicklow, in his jovial tweeds and baggy corduroys, would have had enough heart to help anyone — anyone, that is, who needed the help more than he did himself! However, he did write me a nice letter in which he suggested that I stay on in my good safe job: 'Writers,' he wrote, 'sometimes lose contact with their Muse and come to grief.'

Such wild lunges did however give momentary hope and enabled me to carry on, meanwhile adding a page or two to the already growing pile of works in progress, all incomplete, though started with much fire and fury. The plain truth was that I did not know the first thing about writing: the need for a single clear purpose, for a leisurely, unhurried approach; the drafting and redrafting, writing and rewriting which, though slow and painful, is the one way of getting to the core of what one is trying to say. I was a bit like Belloc's Godolphin, 'always starting things and never ending 'em'! Alas, I didn't have anyone to tell me that even in a good writer's hands inspiration is constantly fading and being rescued, if he's lucky, by the discipline of regular work.

Nevertheless, some things were going in: I was learning to 'hear' what I wrote, to have an ear for speech and the rhythm of words. I began to learn that good writing is hard to write, but easy to read: a lesson that was to stand me in good stead in the most unlikely of places later on, as speech-writer for Tánaiste and Minister for Health Seán MacEntee, who had a most developed sense of style himself, and sought the same in those who worked closely with him.

Meanwhile, such deranged thrusts as the Dunsany and Wicklow appeals did indeed indicate a wish to be in the company of creative people, to hear and talk with them, to be encouraged and confirmed by comparing notes with people of like mind. This was a language I could speak; I would not be happy until my life was caught up wholly with it. I wrote a piece about this and sent it to the poet W. R. Rogers, then a producer with the Third Programme of the BBC; back came five pages of joyous tidings that, with a little adaptation, it could be put on; shortly after, I sent another piece to Roger McHugh, then Professor of English at University College Dublin and friend to many young writers. His reply included a strange phrase that I did not understand then, but which was to prove more and more relevant to my life as I went on: 'Maybe it is your destiny', he wrote, 'to ford the river with the noonday devil on your back!'

The noonday devil had no intention of letting me go. My civil service superiors of those years were decent men trying to do a good and necessary job — no part of which assuredly was to make a writer out of me! I look back with wonderment and admiration at them now and upon their tolerance and forbearance, for literally I would break the heart of a saint. In my favour, however, I suppose I should say that the civil service was not then — I do not know if it is now — very good at encouraging that habit of personal trust, including the possibility of making mistakes, which is at the root of all good working relationships.

'Put the boy on his honour' was a phrase Father would use long ago when some question of truthfulness came up. The civil service was not good at 'putting the boy on his honour'; as such, it sometimes failed quite dismally to develop that personal dynamic that can make even quite ordinary people good, once they are given a chance to see real results for their work.

While all of this was going on, I met the girl I was to marry, and we had a family. She was from a fairly typical Dublin middle-class family: her father, Michael Fagan, an old republican, had refused with De Valera to take the Oath of Allegiance and had lost his job as an agricultural instructor in Donegal because of it. Thereafter, for eleven years, he managed a fruit farm at Kilsallaghan near his native place in Ballyboughal, where my wife-to-be, Margaret, was born. With Dev's coming to power in 1932, he had been reinstated in the civil service, and went on to become Deputy Chief Inspector in the Department of Agriculture. With the change they had moved to Sandymount, and she went to school in Sion Hill in Blackrock, which was what brought us together in the first place. For it so happens that I had gone into digs in Williamstown, opposite Blackrock College, and would pass her on her way to and from school every morning and evening. That went on for quite a while without anything happening. It is hard to write about personal things: all I knew, or seemed to know, was that her eyes dipped devastatingly whenever we passed; was I only thinking that or was it true? I did not know then that there is such a thing as a language of eyes and smiles. Anyway, that whole spring and summer I was studying for my last examination, the one I got first in, and whatever else was on my mind girls were not. Maybe it was the let-up at the end of that tense time that did it, maybe it was going to happen anyway — whatever the cause, on the night I finished we met again, and I spoke to her for the first time. She was on her bicycle, cycling slowly on the footpath with a friend walking along beside her. 'Get down off that bicycle' were the very first words I spoke; the peremptory note was more to give me courage than to intimidate her! Anyway she did as I said, showing an early willingness to put up with my many whims and humours which has gone on for forty years now!

Meanwhile, writing had become central to my life. But first I had to learn something about method.

Another Custom House colleague of those years was Michael Mulvihill, a man who had had his share of trouble in the civil service and elsewhere, but had turned it into fine muscular writing — including *A Sunset Touch*, a sad and beautiful play about the horrors and heroism of the tuberculosis ward.

(Michael had been Noel Browne's private secretary during the famous Mother and Child débâcle.) He it was who taught me that I would have to present my work professionally, properly typed and packaged; that way, at least, it would get over the first hurdle in every editor's life, a disbelief in newcomers! Gradually I began to take it to heart: the writing and rewriting that are essential to good work; the flow that is effortless because your effort was not; the finished work that is easy to read but oh, so hard to write!

Things began to take shape, little things began to happen to give me heart. It was 1956, the year of the Suez crisis; I was twenty-seven; at that age my father had been out there, the Nile, Aden and Alexandria his headquarters. Suez was about oil then; there was a time when it had been about cotton and tea from India and Ceylon. Whatever the connection I found myself writing about William Blake and the 'dark satanic mills' of nineteenth-century England; the piece was published in the *Civil Service Review* and earned me a few guineas.

Shortly afterwards, I wrote a script for the then highly popular 'Balladmakers' Saturday Night' on Radio Éireann; it was accepted. 'The Balladmakers' was a series invented by Michaél Ó hAodha, one of the most underestimated men in the RTE of his time. It had some fine contributors: Bryan MacMahon, who pioneered the idea, Sigerson Clifford (*The Boys of Barr na Sráide*), Brendan Behan, Ben Kiely and Seán Óg Ó Tuama had all written for it. It was quite something to be in such talented company.

Then a job came up in radio. It was a local service to be opened in Cork; I applied and, though without broadcasting experience, the letter of rejection I got said I could indeed think about a future in broadcasting because I appeared to have a feel for the broadcasting scene. Was I on the right track at last? In spite of the failures and rejections, if I continued could I eventually dare hope to succeed?

That winter I developed one of my rare bouts of illness and was sent off to hospital; it was nothing more than appendicitis but it meant six weeks free from work. On my first day home, I took out some of my old script rejects and began to re-work them. With the hindsight rewriting brings, I could see now that they had a certain core that the writing had only imperfectly brought out. So I began again, cutting, polishing, re-shaping, until at long last I had them as I thought right. By then the six weeks were up and I sent them off — one to *The Sign* in New Jersey, the other to the BBC — and went back then to my humdrum life.

It was mid-February, the snowdrops were out, there was a touch of spring in the air, but my spring was over; it had lasted the six weeks of my sabbatical; it would not come back! There was now a family to keep, the job I had was the one way I could keep them; writing was a pipe-dream, living by it worse — far better writers than I couldn't do it. Those recent things I had finished and was pleased with because I had been able to give them time, even they would in all probability come back, come thumping through the letterbox as all the others before had come, a few more clunking rejects on the gathering pile of an aborted life! I was close on thirty, my future, like my past, behind me. From now on, I could settle for the one role left to me, that of local boy made good — for nothing!

Then, one night coming up to Easter, I came home and the house was in darkness. When I came in, there was an envelope in the hall: not the usual bulky reject but a slim white envelope with an American postmark. Need I say more? The cheque — it was five hundred dollars — was not money: I never wanted to cash it at all! I wanted to keep it and show it, the living proof that the years of the rejects and failures had been worth while. A few days later, another letter arrived, this time from a man called L. Lockhart Kriel, a producer with the Talks Department of the BBC — for whose soul, be he living or dead, I pray eternal happiness, for it brought tidings of even greater joy: acceptance of the talk I had sent them, and a request to send six more!

So 'goodbye little yellow bird, I'd rather brave the cold in a world that's free, than a prisoner be in a cage of gold!' Maybe at long last I could begin!

8

THE LITTLE WHITE ROSE
OF SCOTLAND

IT WAS clear now that whatever it was that had turned me to
writing in the first place would remain; but equally clear that,
with five children to keep — we eventually ended up with
eight — I would have to stick with the only paid job I had. I had
now been in the civil service for ten years and was still as far
as ever from being happy there; then suddenly everything
changed. What probably triggered this off was a play I had
written for the Abbey and for which I had entertained high
hopes. It was called *And Never Fall* — the phrase was from that
old song of my mother's, *All Around the Shanty Table* — and told
the story of an Irish emigrant in London who had been caught
up in a robbery and murder. It had an exaggerated plot, no
character worth talking about (apart from one Bethseda who
was to turn up in other work later on and was an amalgam of all
the strong and passionate women of my childhood), and a great
deal of moral preaching, largely derived from the then current
vogue of Colin Winson's 'Angry Young Men' and John
Osborne's *Look Back in Anger*.

I waited patient months for the play to come back. As time
went by, I convinced myself that it would not come back, that
delay meant acceptance, not rejection, this time. It did not.
When eventually the rejection came, it was stunningly final. In a
brief conversation with Ernest Blythe, then Managing Director,
he informed me with characteristic bluntness that, whatever else
I might be, a playwright I was not.

It was at this crucial point that Pádraig de Burca and Willie
O'Reilly arrived as superiors into my civil service life; both of them
were men I greatly liked.

Paddy was a jovial fellow of rakish gait and consuming
volubility, but with a fine mind through all his talk. He had been

appointed an administrative officer in 1953 on an intake that included Declan Brennan and Maurice Doyle, now Secretaries respectively of the Departments of Education and Finance. Paddy might have been more successful had he stayed where he started, which was Finance, but Health was a growing department in those years, and he as well as others felt that he would have much better chances there. When I met him, he was already studying for an MA in Celtic Studies under Tomás de Bhaldraithe; he was also involved with studies in administration, which would subsequently take him on an exchange fellowship to Pittsburgh, including a stint on management with General Motors, an absorbing experience from which he never wholly recovered.

In those early days, he did little but talk — and what talk! It was a delight to get him in full spate, and he was in full spate often. The trouble was that he was rarely in anything else. The more scintillating the conversation, the less the work-rate; and with our mutual boss a man of stern stuff, this was a sure-fire course for disaster. His luminous philosophy would comfortably take us through the morning tea-break right up to midday; on a 'good' day right up until it was time to go home. I began to wonder when, if ever, the job we had to do would get done; more to the point, since he showed no signs of doing it, who was going to do it, if not I!

That was the beginning: I simply could not let down this delightful young man whom I liked so much; so at home at nights or in the early mornings before he got in, I would get going myself and finish off as much as I could, to the point where he had little to do but put his name to it — thus leaving him free to carry on with what he was really good at!

We worked on legislation, a complex area requiring much care and attention; as it happened, there was right then a large programme to be put through the Oireachtas in the coming sessions. There was a Bill to regulate the practice of pharmacy; another to set up a comprehensive system for the control of poisons. A legislative loophole existed whereby foreign doctors could not practise in Ireland — that had to be amended; nurses' legislation was also in course of preparation. Finally, there was a Bill to institute new controls over corporate bodies in the health field: a large and contentious area. When he became Minister for Health, Seán MacEntee was already on old man, and Health

74

was thought to be a quiet department where he could sit back and retire in comfort while still holding full ministerial office. The reality was quite different: no sooner was he installed than the firmament began to shake. He himself was a brilliant administrator, with close on half a century of experience behind him. Had he not been a politician he would have made a superb civil servant himself. This meant that he set standards for his civil servants which only the highest quality would reach: clarity of mind and thought, a style in presentation, negotiating skills, and a probity born of unabated national dedication. Finally, he required a degree of accuracy that left no room for the sloppy or the slipshod in the whole working scene. In this service one had to be permanently on one's toes.

Yet here was I day by day in this demanding scene with a young master — he was an administrative officer, I still an executive — who wanted to talk nothing but Tolstoy and Turgenev and the myths of ancient Greece all day long!

The crunch came one day when, pressed into action, the talk temporarily ceased and he picked up the dictaphone to do a speech on one of the forthcoming Bills. This one was about the control of drugs; I was sitting at a desk near him and could hear everything. Now it so happens that I had made myself quite knowledgeable on this subject, and subsequently became Secretary of the first Council set up under the Bill — the Chairman being Desmond O'Malley (father of the Progressive Democrats' Des whom I used to meet occasionally when he came in as a penurious law student, begging, I imagine, the usual few bob from an indulgent father, during our monthly lunch in the Hibernian). This Bill was to set up the Council, describe its functions and lay down the general lines on which the whole traffic in drugs and poisons would run. It was a good practical measure requiring a good practical speech. But what I heard on the dictaphone that day was very far from that. It was a discourse on the history of drugs in the life of humanity — Socrates with his hemlock in ancient Greece was there; Tarquinius Superbus and the arsenic taken in small doses to foil his poisoners when they came; King Hamlet, poisoned through the earhole by his brother as he slept in the garden in Elsinore. I could could see it coming! The deadline was past, there was no time for change or revision now. When the Tánaiste and Minister for Health said he wanted something by a certain time, he meant that time, not a moment later. So the magnum opus was typed and brought in to our stern master.

Those cartoons of Tom and Jerry and the Pink Panther best illustrate what happened next. The walls seemed to shake with fury; I just sat there helpless, expecting the door to burst open. When he came out, his face was ashen and his mouth open as if he had lost control of his facial muscles. The boss's point was undoubtedly that the only way he would ever learn was by being pushed in at the deep end like that; in this, bearing in mind the lord and master *he* had to face with Paddy's fanciful pot-pourri, he showed commendable trust not alone in the delegation system but in the inadequate, not to say hare-brained, instruments with which he had to implement it. But with no offence to him and at this lengthy remove, I believe I can in all sincerity say that that moment had a most serious effect upon the rest of Paddy's short life.

'What happened?' I asked, hoping by my apparent ease to pretend I had not noticed. 'He didn't like it!' he said. I was too fond of him to go on pretending. 'Maybe it's not factual enough,' I ventured. 'Why don't you try again? Get a new slant on it, a more practical one?' 'I can't do any more to the damn thing,' he moaned miserably. 'Everything I know about the bloody subject is there!'

It was true; but what was also true — I could see his point — was that not a single word of it could be used. 'Maybe if you forgot the history,' I suggested, 'and tried to say something practical about the Bill?' 'Would you try it?' he brightened. 'Maybe you'd be able to work in a few things of your own.'

I might have known it would be like this; in fact I did know, and only the previous night had written 'a few things of my own' in anticipation of this very moment. I got them together hastily now — it is not for nothing one spends years writing and rewriting — and gave it to him to hand in the following day. The stern man was pleased: clearly his method of reproof had worked! He was a good and able man, one who sensibly believed in making square pegs fit round holes, since they were the only pegs he had. Later on, he was to become a first-class Secretary of the department — and incidentally taught me a great deal of what I know about legislative and governmental affairs. But so far as the narrative in these pages is concerned, his main function was by his very toughness to help turn two marked failures into one moderate success. I think of him now as a highly competent public servant doing good and necessary work; while with Paddy I think of his talk and his laughter and his consuming intellectual life, things that make the company of some human beings a constant source of stimulus and delight.

When he died, as he did only a few years later at the impossible age of thirty-four, I thought of his wild and fumbling efforts to come to grips with the tedious world of the real, and of his all but total failure to do so. But I loved him as I would a brother; and that made up for a lot. He was the least lugubrious of people, but he *would* go and die on Christmas Eve, which means that every year that passes I can never forget his death. There were only a few of us to follow his body down to Dungarvan, where he had been born — Tom Barrington, Des Roche, Bill Smith and Jim O'Donnell, all from the Institute of Public Administration where he had gone to work by then. Never have I been at a more desolate funeral. Sleet swept in sheets across the bay from Helvick and the little villages of the Ring Gaeltacht where they still spoke the Irish language which he loved. It was as if he had carried all the fun and laughter in the world out of it along with him. I often thought that if I could have stayed in the place instead of leaving as I did, it might have made a difference to his life. It would have been a debt repaid; he had certainly helped remake mine.

Willie O'Reilly was very different from Paddy, quiet and reflective as Paddy was vociferous and loud. He communicated a sense of living at a remove from life, as if all that were some sort of good-natured charade. Before I met him he had been largely responsible for a massive Mental Health Bill, had been private secretary to Tom O'Higgins in the second Coalition, and subsequently — which was quite unusual, bearing in mind political preferments — to Seán MacEntee. He had the reputation for being one hundred per cent trustworthy, a reputation which, despite a boyish face, may have derived from his self-made triad of nullities: 'I am nothing, I have nothing, I can do nothing.'

He used to tell a story about sheep. A civil servant is passing a field in the company of two others — a bank clerk, say, and a lawyer — where they see some newly shorn sheep. It is early spring, and the bank clerk remarks: 'Those sheep have been shorn.' The lawyer agrees and adds: 'It's early in the year for that.' But the true-born civil servant, a Doubting Thomas to the core, believes only the evidence of his eyes: 'Yes,' he agrees, 'on this side at least!'

He would tell this story against himself, but the lesson did not go astray on me: a rigorous pursuit of the facts and a cold assessment of the facts had not up to that been the strongest suit in my life. But there was more to him than that. One day I brought him in some papers to sign. In the normal course, following the 'shorn sheep' model, I thought he would first read them carefully before signing; instead, he just glanced rapidly over the page and put his name to it — a name which, as I say, meant that whatever went above it was one hundred per cent correct. My first thought was to ask him to withdraw it, to hold it at least until he had read more carefully what I had done; but clearly he did not want that. The effect of such total trust was alarming. I took what I had done away with me, checked and double-checked it this time to make sure it was right — to be able to say with his kind of absolute finality that there was no square inch of that sheep, seen or unseen, that wasn't shorn. So the man who 'could do nothing' had done with me in ten seconds what others had failed to do in ten years.

There were other sides to him. He had a consuming interest in mathematics, and would occasionally show me what seemed to me highly erudite papers, which I couldn't make head or tail of, having no interest in the subject myself. More to my taste was his interest in literature. He read widely and discriminatingly and remembered what he read. He had a strong affection for Chekhov — 'a writer', he prophetically told me, 'for the maturer years.' The other Russians — Tolstoy, Dostoievsky, even Turgenev — did not make the same appeal; they were all-black, all-white, unlike life, which is mostly a shade between. Quietly, through the traumas of his own official years, he had come to a cold assessment of his place in the world, not much of a place but sufficient for him, leaving it to others about him to strive all they liked, provided they left him alone.

His modesty was well rewarded. To achieve the first of his famous triad — 'I am nothing' — he removed himself by early retirement from the service shortly after I left, and thereafter, whenever asked what he was, could in all honesty reply, 'I am nothing.' The second he achieved in an equally unobtrusive but effective way: his astute and cautious mind had made a hobby of the stock exchange, which benevolent institution, though he was now without job or income, enables him to say very comfortably to this day, 'I have nothing.' As to the third — 'I can do nothing' — when I see him now, as I sometimes do, sauntering ruminatively along the sea road at Booterstown, or wheeling his grandchild out in the pram as wise men may do, I think to myself how incredibly astute and long-headed some innocent-seeming people may be!

My first real associations with the language were almost completely by chance. Séamus Ó Dúgáin worked in the Department of Local Government in the Custom House, and for years after I left school and came to work there he was to be the sole living link I had with the spoken word. He taught me a great deal of what I know about it, as well as leading me, by his discerning and well-stocked mind, to the important literary sources.

In those years of the late fifties and early sixties another of the Custom House tea-break coterie was Richard Power, who later went on to write a fine novel called *The Hungry Grass* but right then was celebrating the success of a lovely book in Irish called *Úll i mBarr an Ghéagáin* ('Apple in the Treetop'). It was about a spell he had spent in the Aran Islands in 1957; he had had the wit to use the widely trumpeted official favour towards the language to get himself a sabbatical to go there to hear the native speech and so help him with his work. The following year I went to Aran too; not on a sabbatical — one swallow had made *that* summer, the civil service saw to that! — but because Dick's book had impressed me so much. It was my first real brush with the living language since leaving school. Surprisingly, I managed fairly well, apart from odd words and phrases and the usual experience in longer conversations when I seemed to run out of steam. The pubs at night were a mecca for everyone, visitors and locals alike; without the same Gaeltacht pubs, where there is at least an atmosphere of cordiality in which the learner's inhibitions break down, I believe the language would be in a far weaker state than it is.

It was in one of those pubs — Seán a' Chreige's near Fearann an Choirce in Inishmore — that I first heard some of the lovely Irish songs: to someone brought up as I was on John McCormack, Nelson Eddy, and Sidney MacEwen it was new and exciting, something far closer to the Irish mind and heart. One night, a girl came in from Connemara across the bay. Later on I would get to know her well: she was Beryl Cunningham

from Carraroe — one of the lovely sean-nós singers. A few weeks
before she died in Saint Luke's Hospital in Dublin many years
later, I recalled that first night when I met her as, from the far
end of the smoke-filled room she began to sing a song I had not
heard before. The place was packed; a moment previously there
had been a great babble of noise, but suddenly, as her lone voice
rose in the air, a silence fell upon the place. The song was *An Clár
Bog Déil* ('The Soft Deal Board'), a Munster love-song with a
haunting air:

> Do phósfainn thú, gan bó gan punt, gan áireamh spré,
> A chuid den tsaol le toil do mhuintire, dá mb'áil leat é;
> Sé mo ghalar dubhach gan mé 'gus tú, a ghrá mo chlé,
> I gCaiseal Mumhan, is gan de leaba fúinn ach an clár
>   bog déil.

> I'd marry you, my part of life, and neither kith nor kine
> Shall ever turn my heart from you, for you alone are
>   mine.
> I'd gladly trade my health and wealth — yes, all I can
>   afford,
> To lay my head upon your bed on Cashel's soft deal
>   board

Each time after that I heard such a song, a new glory of a lost
civilisation awoke, a new fragment of Irish life was re-created
and restored as slowly, gradually, a new me was beginning to be
born.

That year a new book in Irish came out; it was called
Scéalaíocht na Ríthe ('Sagas of the Kings'). It was a set of epic tales
from medieval times done into modern Irish by Professor
Proinsias Mac Cana and Tomás Ó Floinn. Much of what I had
done at school was dull stuff, thin in plot, weak to non-existent in
character: *Scéalaíocht na Ríthe* was different from that. Here were
stories of real flesh and blood, of depth and dignity, with neither
pretence nor imitation nor anything at all shallow or maudlin or
indulgent about them. Here was a people with a code of mores
and behaviour distinctively and proudly their own; a separate
and confident people moving surefootedly in a mould of life
that was unbroken for long centuries, a people who did not have
to rely on caricature or patois or a bogus and over-projected
sense of national identity for effect. It was a book with that rarest

80

of rare things in Irish cultural life, aristocracy of the mind. If I am pressed to make comparisons with it in modern work, I do not find them here at all but must look outside Ireland, to Sigrid Undset's great novel about medieval Norway, *Kristin Lavransdatter,* or to stories of classic bravery like Gogol's *Taras Bulba,* and *White Cavalry* by Isaac Babel, about life in Cossack Russia.

Whatever it was, I passionately wanted to absorb and belong to it; what was more, I wanted others to belong to it too. Quite literally, I loved it for the uplift and nobility of mind it brought to the worn-out and dried-up cultural atmosphere of my own time. And I wanted to spread and share the knowledge of it with Irish people everywhere, so as to make the whole shabby, material-minded, mentally poverty-stricken generation of our time recognise the pearl of great price that was ours for the asking but which we did not seem to want at all.

How could such a message be got across? How could ordinary people, with hardly enough time and less mind to read the daily paper, be got to understand all that? And if they could not, must it then be lost forever? Was there nothing at all any of us alive and appreciative of it could do to bring it back?

Meanwhile, I had a life to live and children of my own to rear. Some time before all this, our eldest child had gone to school. Partly because it was near home, partly because it was a national school, we sent her to Scoil Lorcáin, an all-Irish school in Monkstown, near Dún Laoghaire. Many such schools have grown up since, but at that time Scoil Lorcáin was unique in that it was the sole one of its kind that had been set up in recent times. From the very start, it was to have a profound influence upon us. It wasn't only the children who learnt there, the parents did too; daily contact with those marvellous dedicated teachers of the early years of Scoil Lorcáin made the language a real and living reality in our lives. Bean Uí Chadhain — the writer Máirtín Ó Cadhain's wife — had been a learner of Irish herself and knew well what the learner's problems were: that they learn best when not intimidated; that fluency is achieved by stages, as a child learns to walk. To hear Bean Uí Chadhain bring little children from completely English-speaking homes through their first words in Irish, always conscious of the mothers and fathers who came to deliver or collect them and who were listening, was an object lesson for all emergent nations that have suffered a language loss, in how that language can be restored.

One day, a few months after she had started school, our own little girl began to pipe up at the dinner table:

> Rinne síóg píóg lá amháin i gcóir an rí,
> Agus céard a bhí faoin gcrústa ach éiníní beaga buí!
> Nuair a chuir sí ins an oighean í, bhí spraoi is spórt ansin,
> Mar thosaigh chuile éinín ag portaíocht go binn!

The sounds were perfect, and from the remains of my half-forgotten school Irish I instantly recognised it:

> When the pie was opened, the birds began to sing;
> Wasn't it the dainty dish to set before the king!

That nursery rhyme of Bean Uí Chadhain's became the first words of living Irish spoken in our house. It was nothing; yet from it everything came. Dr T. K. Whitaker's First Programme for Economic Expansion had been launched, the burgeoning sixties were on their way; it was a time of high hope and high endeavour in Ireland. In the world generally people were looking for their roots and finding them; and in the joy and pride of that new self-knowledge, a new self-confidence was being born. In my own life, I began to ask myself if from such tiny beginnings a whole new rich bilingual idiom could be brought about, whether the same could not be got to happen for all the other families who might want it all over the country?

What could make it happen? What could awaken people's interest sufficiently to make this not just my experience alone but the experience of every new family growing up now in Ireland? Little did I think that before long I would become involved in trying to find the answer.

One result of this new upsurge of language vitality was that I began to write more in Irish. There were no great rewards there, but at least you could be pretty sure of being published — and publication is what writing is about. Despite Ernest Blythe's earlier rejection, I even began to write a play in Irish, though I knew that, if successful, it would be seen by no more than a few hundred people. Somehow, the numbers didn't seem to count; once they were people of discernment who knew what one was at, the satisfaction would be just the same. The tiny Damer Hall in Stephen's Green had a fine group of amateur actors and an inspiring director in Frank Dermody; Brendan Behan had first written *The Hostage* in Irish for it. To be in that company was a distinction in itself.

Behan was a most sincere language man — though he couldn't stand the posturing and 'piosity' of some of its more ardent adherents. It was good to be in his company in the Forty-Foot during the good years when he wasn't drunk or trying to put on an act.

All my life since coming to Dublin in 1947 I have been a swimmer in the same Forty-Foot in Sandycove where I still go, summer and winter, almost every day of my life. The Forty-Foot is a most democratic place where, over the years, one met all sorts of people, from politicians like President Hillery; Dr Noel Browne; ex-Taoiseach John A. Costello and his son, Declan, now a judge; David Andrews and Michael O'Kennedy; to well-known actors and performers like Cyril Cusack and Frank Kelly. Nobody bothers much with class; the bus-conductors, carpenters, bricklayers and unemployed who sit around after a swim are every bit as much a part of the scene as the well known. Behan could never seem to make up his mind which company he wanted to be in. He would have been more at home with the plain people, yet there was a hankering after the 'big' names too. If there was a priest in the company — which in the Forty-Foot there often is, only you can't tell because he's not wearing his clothes — he would become particularly vociferous. He always spoke Irish to me which, to say the least, was unusual in the Forty-Foot in those days.

One day when we were chatting away quietly about something or other, an elderly man beside us got up and went over to get his clothes to dress. It so happens I knew him well: he was Canon Troy of Ballyfermot, a thoroughly decent and inoffensive man. But the minute Brendan saw the black cloth and red stock he dropped the Irish and let fly on the multiple evils of the Church in Ireland. It would have been no good trying to reason with him, he was in full flight. Suddenly he was on to Monsignor Pádraig de Brún of Galway who, as it happens, had been a friend of Canon Troy's, but whom Brendan had met in the company of Kruger Kavanagh during his time in Dún Chaoin. There, he said, was a scholar and a true-born Irishman — 'not like the rest of the creeps, the only fuckin' priest worth a curse since John MacHale of Tuam — and signs on it, he was preached off the altar in the craw-thumping Senate of Ireland for it!' Then, as if to substantiate his assessment of the hierarchy, he went on to quote his own translation of the medieval Irish quatrain that Monsignor de Brún had taught him and which finds specific and ribald cause for the origins of English Protestantism:

> Don't speak of the alien Minister
> Nor his church without meaning nor faith,
> For the foundation-stone of his temple
> Was the ballocks of Henry the Eighth!

Poor Canon Troy left shortly afterwards with his handsome red setter. He was a gentle and humorous man, and I think he enjoyed the performance hugely. Behan turned back to me and reverted to Irish. That day's quantum of invective was spun out!

It was about this time that another name began to be mentioned, somebody I had known in my brief time at university in Cork — then a thin and weedy youth, smoking cheroots and affecting an oriental goatee: reedy by name and by nature! This John Reidy had gone on to qualify in music, and had actually for a time become a most unlikely Assistant Director of Music in Radio Éireann. But he had given all that up as a bad job and gone to live in Paris with his wife, Ruth, where he went through the motions of the Left Bank before coming back to Dublin in the mid-fifties, which was when I next met him. This was in the company of another friend, then also in the bondage of civil servitude, the poet Thomas Kinsella. Tom introduced him to me as Seán Ó Riada. His story was exactly the same as my own: he too had sent his children to Scoil Lorcáin, and was to become yet one more example of the seminal importance of that school in making the language and its associated culture a vital creative element in a family's life.

Whether he could afford it or not — and he could not! — he lived like a prince, and had a princely sense of what national dignity and national aspirations should be about. How he managed to live so well was a mystery. Back in Ireland he got a small job with a big name: he was Director of Music at the Abbey Theatre, where he had two other musicians besides himself to direct! We would see him in the pit directing his trio from the piano with the fire and style of a Mahler. By now he had a mane of reddish hair and, instead of the goatee, a

84

moustache, which gave him an extraordinarily elegant look. There were always groups of traditional musicians gathering in the basement of his house at Galloping Green in Stillorgan, including the now world-famous Chieftains whom he had first brought together to perform in an Abbey play by Bryan MacMahon. But none of this led us to expect that what the language, the traditional music and all the rejected security were leading up to was the magnificent cathartic explosion of the film music for *Mise Éire* upon the whole emergent cultural scene.

Mise Éire was a film produced by George Morrison from archival material — old newsreel, stills and newspaper cuttings — about the period from the foundation of Sinn Féin at the turn of the century, through 1916, up to the landslide general election of 1919. It was highly evocative material, carefully chosen and brilliantly put together; but what made it, what put it away ahead of all other archive-based Irish documentaries before or since was Ó Riada's inspired and sublime musical score.

The timing was also relevant. It came in the wake of one of the bleakest periods in Irish economic history. In 1958 came that First Programme for Economic Expansion already mentioned, masterminded by Dr T. K. Whitaker for Minister for Finance Dr Jim Ryan and newly elected Taoiseach Seán Lemass. There was movement in the air, a new stirring of old roots. Once again there seemed to be a possibility of hope. The previous year had been a black one for everyone: the emigration figures were catastrophic; it seemed only a matter of time until everyone would be gone. Then, suddenly, came this new statement of national economic aims, a new and confident prediction that better times were on the way. For that there would be need for confidence, courage, patriotism and hard work. I don't know how much, if any, of that was in Ó Riada's mind — although I do know that his sense of patriotic commitment was deep and real. What is certain is that, with the music of *Mise Éire* all our hearts were instantly stirred.

What Dvořák had done for Czechoslovakia, Chopin for Poland, Smetana for Romania, and Sibelius for Finland, Seán Ó Riada with *Mise Éire* did for us in Ireland. It was a crucible of the nation's dreams, its griefs and joys, its martyrdom and sublimation, swelling to the concluding titanic rapture of *Róisín*

Dubh — an Ireland of hope and glory yet to come. There were hundreds of balladeers about, thousands of traditional musicians and groups, but their music and singing was repetitious stuff, it had been done before and would be undoubtedly done again; but this statement in music of the Irish dream, without a word being spoken, did for us what words could never do: it established a new awareness, a new sense of pride in our own place and its people, a new dedication to see that pride fulfilled. It was our *Cry, the Beloved Country* and went straight to the heart. Those of us so inspired by it could not but be moved to lend a hand in building a new sense of national self-esteem. We were the first educated generation of freedom: *Mise Éire* called us to a sense of idealistic purpose that would make that freedom worth while.

It was Ó Riada in a way who first brought me to Kerry. He had left the job with the grandiose title in Dublin. Dick Power and I were with him in the Abbey at a play of Dick's on his last night, and afterwards we went round to the Abbey Mooney for a drink. He was fed up, he said, with the whole rotten Dublin round; there were too many phoneys and fanatics about, too many false prophets, too much unnecessary politics. Yeats was right: 'Much hatred, little room'! He was going to Kerry, to Ballyferriter in the heartland of the Gaeltacht; he was bringing the family with him, lock, stock and barrel; and he would not be back. The language had become central to his life now. Unlike most of us who had been caught up with it, he was carrying it to its logical conclusion; he was going back to the roots that had started a whole new world of creativity for him, and he would live as best he could from there.

Some weeks later I met him with Ruth one night, walking the road between Ballyferriter and Dún Chaoin. He was avoiding the 'stróinséirí' — the holiday visitors — and scarcely came to the village at all. I was reminded of Vaughan Williams, a bitter exile on the northern moors, hearing his sublime music put to jingoistic words; reminded too, as I looked at this man who had made music of epic proportions out of 'Róisín Dubh', the little dark rose of Ireland, of the Scots poet, Hugh MacDiarmid, writing of the imperilled culture of his own people: 'Not for me the great roses of all the world, for me the little white rose of Scotland that smells sweetly and breaks the heart.'

What was breaking my heart right then was the play in Irish I was trying to write for the Damer. Of all forms of writing, drama has to be the most difficult for the non-native speaker; even a great writer like Beckett in *Godot* was still, to some extent, inventing speech — though at least he had the advantage of hearing French all around him as he wrote. But by now I had another advantage, that of habit; good, bad or indifferent, two pages of finished typescript came out of that typewriter every night. That was while I was in Dublin; now, hearing the living speech of the Gaeltacht all around me, the pace doubled. The characters in the play became like Joan of Arc's 'voices'; I could hear them in my head as I wrote. The result was that the play I had hoped to advance by an act at most while in Ballyferriter was finished by the time the fortnight was up.

The day I was leaving I met Ó Riada in the local pub where he came in to get the daily paper. When I told him I was leaving he looked at me out of those cavalier eyes — at that time he was 'high' on the poetry of Piaras Feirtéir, the bandit prince hanged at Killarney in 1653, when Ireland was at its lowest. 'Níl tú ag dul aon áit,' he said, 'tá tú ag fanúint anseo!' ('You're going nowhere, you're staying here'). I protested that I couldn't stay, I had no accommodation; and he protested, even more strongly, that I could because he would find it for me! What followed, as we stopped and enquired in every second house between the two villages, was a riot of songs and music and poetry, of old stories with new friends, a voyage of discovery into a vastly rich and exciting, if materially disfranchised, world. He found me the accommodation, and it was a fortnight later by the time we left, I promising to read the poems of Piaras Feirtéir, he the fine new history of the Famine, *The Great Hunger,* brought out by Cecil Woodham-Smith just then. We would meet again in Dublin in a month to compare notes. Our devoted wives — we had families the same age who had been in the same classes at Scoil Lorcáin together — looked at each other in mutual dismay; it was perhaps as well that henceforth there would be hundreds of miles between us!

My play won an Irish-language drama award for that year. It was called *Spéir Thóirní* ('A Thunder Cloud') and was about an Indian girl at university in Dublin who had fallen in love with an Irish boy, but his mother would not have her in the house. The punch-line came when she confronted her with the word 'half-caste!' It was based on an incident from real life. I knew the girl — she was beautiful and sophisticated — and her dull boy-friend: it was when you saw the two of them together that you realised which of the two was gaining and which losing, if ever they made a match. I had lived with the theme for several months, and having got it out of my system at last, I thought it might be a while before I tried another play again. Such resolutions happily do not last; by the time I got news that it had won the Oireachtas drama award for that year, I had all but forgotten it and was on to another.

Lying in bed in my old home in Cork one morning, the idea for this play came to me. Half-way between waking and sleeping, I heard the children, my own children, playing downstairs; but, in that moment between sleep and consciousness, it suddenly seemed to me that it was not they who were there at all, but my own brothers and sisters, as we had all been long ago, long before we had all grown up and gone our separate ways. What had life done to us since? What strangeness had come along to separate us and our lives, each of us now living on our own, cut off from all the others? What were the griefs and failures, the sorrows and joys, the pains and losses, by now even the deaths, that had come to break us apart and separate us, as happened to all families — to make us different from what we were, we who never felt we could be separated at all? I woke, half-crying with the fore-knowledge of all that was to come; I knew I would get no peace until I had written it all down. I believe I had the core of the play in that first waking moment; whenever, in the coming months while I was working on it, I faltered, I had only to go back and recall that initial sense of grief to push me on. True, I was helped on the way by some fine examples of similar plays — Tenessee Williams's *The Glass Menagerie* and Thornton Wilder's *Our Town*; perhaps above all by *Time and the Conways*, a marvellous play by that much-underestimated writer J. B. Priestley, about the tragedy of time in people's lives; but the bedrock was my own experience on that first waking morning.

The play — it was called *In Iothlainn Dé* (a phrase from the poem *Ag Críost an Síol*) — went on to win an Irish Life Award the following year; but by then my whole life had changed again. For by now I was really into the civil service in a big way.

Now that I had at last come to grips with it and really knew what I was doing, I was pushed out in front more, something that did not displease me at all. Civil servants need a great deal more of that: being conscientious people, but reticent at heart, they often know their subject well but are slow and tentative at putting it across. A busy Minister above all needs that; he is the one who is going to have to get out in public and explain what it is all about; he cannot possibly have it all written down. Even when it is, some of them can still make a fair stab at making a mess of it!

For what it's worth, I may say a word in parenthesis here about some of them. Dr Noël Browne of the ill-fated Mother and Child Scheme was loved by the staff as no other Minister I have ever known was loved; but, though a concerned reformer and passionately committed to his work, he was headstrong and wilful and in the end, as was increasingly to emerge over the ensuing years, did not have the skills needed for political and administrative life in Ireland. Dr Jim Ryan, on the other hand, was deceptively easygoing but was still a man, when tested, who had all the idealism and dedication of his early revolutionary days: he was the final-year medical student who had attended the wounded James Connolly in the GPO in 1916; and in all his subsequent health and social welfare thinking he never lost sight of Connolly's socialist thrust. Tom O'Higgins, ex-Chief Justice and now Judge of the European Court, was single-minded and forthright to the point of dismissiveness, and when he wanted something done, as he did with the now universally applauded Voluntary Health Insurance scheme, it was 'Yes, Minister' all the way. Seán MacEntee was an old man by the time I met him but he was quite the most energetic Minister of them all, as well as being, contrary to the common report, the most gracious and charming of men — far too fastidious, I am bound to say, for much of the cattle-jobber side of Irish political life! Finally there was Charles Haughey, one of the younger breed who crossed my line of vision briefly when, as Minister for Justice, he was putting through his Intoxicating Liquor Bill in the early sixties — the Department of Health being responsible for advising on the blood-level tolerance. I could see even then that he was an exceptional man; he had a style and ease of bearing which was born of real confidence — he actually walked with a strut, as of someone who is in no rush because he knows where he is going and is in no hurry to get there. He could turn on charm like a light, but when at work he was monosyllabic and direct to the point of truculence; spades were spades, no matter what fine company might be about. This was a tremendous help when it came to the crucial business of decision-making. There was no doubting the sagacity and surefootedness of his mature political mind. It did not surprise me that this rich array of talents should lead to stardom later on, including, inevitably, the stardom of trouble; but I am equally certain that he still knows how to assess all the facts of a given situation and to make wise and timely judgements as to how what he wants achieved is to be done.

Most of these people might have had some nodding acquaintance with the anonymous official I then was up and down the corridors of power; but certain it is that none of them would have had the slightest inkling that I was living another, wholly different, life (nor, indeed, cared!) The spiral-bound notebooks in which I did my drafting were doubly active now: as I walked across Killiney Hill overlooking Dublin Bay in the evenings, they would become steadily filled, on one side with notes for a Second Reading speech or committee debate; on the other, with bits and pieces of dialogue, stage notes, hints and pointers to characters in the play on which I was at work. There was an extraordinary complementarity between them: I seemed to be on a pendulum swing between both, each swing demanding the other in perfect ease and harmony. Ever since, I have been sceptical about the appropriation of the word 'creative' by the so-called creative arts, as if it were some sort of exclusive preserve. The last thing the creative spirit is is élitist; on the contrary, it responds to all the creative urges, whether they be in the limited field of the arts themselves or in those wider fields of life in general, where creativity in a whole variety of forms is constantly being evoked.

It was into the middle of this now highly satisfactory situation that my friend Dick Power put a casual question to me one morning as we were going in on the train. Would I, he asked, be applying for 'the job'? 'What job?' I asked blankly; I didn't know of any. 'The one in the papers this morning,' he told me. 'It's for an Editor of Irish Language Television Programmes in RTE.' I looked at him whimsically: Dick had a wry sense of humour of his own! 'Indeed I'm not,' I said. 'As you know better than anyone, I spent long enough trying to get to grips with what I'm at without ruining the whole thing now for something I don't want!'

That, so far as I was concerned, was that; even if I had thought of it, the fact is I wouldn't have had a chance. True, the language, and how to advance it, had become central to my life; also, as a writer and journalist I had done some few things that might merit attention. But how could someone who knew nothing about television except to look at the screen expect to be considered for a job in so highly technical a field?

Television in Ireland then was a strange new trade: slick, meretricious, an attractor of mid-Atlantic smoothies! Whoever else it was meant for, it wasn't meant for me! There was a further point: to those of us on the outside, Radio Éireann at that time seemed a closed shop, where everyone knew everyone else and automatically gave each other advantage when it came to filling jobs. What chance could a newcomer like me have in such company? So no sooner had Dick Power said what he had said and I had given my answer than the whole thing was wiped from my mind. But it was not to be so.

The turning point came in the form of a telephone call from a man called Breandán Ó Huallacháin, a teacher and part-time journalist with whom I had become friendly because of my holiday associations with his home place in Leataobh Mór near Ballyferriter in Kerry. He had seen the advertisement in the newspapers and wanted my advice on how to go about applying. He knew I was an administrator, assumed I would be interested — and when he found I was not, was delighted to be able to pick my brains. I was, of course, glad to help: he was a good man, keen on the language too; so I told him as best I could what he should do: the documents to read, the studies to make, the questions to anticipate, and the considered, informed answers to have ready to give.

The conversation lasted a long time, well over an hour I'm sure, and when I had finished, my wife, who happened to be within earshot and hence heard it all, said something that, like Dick Power's earlier remark, was to have a profound effect on my life. 'If you believe some of the things you've been saying about the language,' she said, 'you ought to go and get that job. You really are the man for it!'

Like love or death or the first hint of a final parting, I knew in that instant that it would happen. There is a kind of providence in such things. I suppose I could not have gone on as I was — one or other of the two streams would have dried up. I did not want the 'creative' side to go, yet that was the more likely; neither did I want the administrator in me to stop, a skill I had come to learn lately and which I now greatly enjoyed. That night I put pen to paper and, true to form, I did not do it by halves.

The interview board chairman, when it was held, was Roibeard Ó Faracháin, a poet and writer of worth himself and at that time Controller of Radio Programmes; with him were John Irvine, Head of Administration, a man I did not know at the time but was subsequently to come to know extremely well; Pádraic Ó Raghallaigh, who at that time was Assistant Controller of Television Programmes, but whom everyone knew better for his magnificent voice (he, with Liam Budhlaeir, had done the voice-over for *Mise Éire*); Jack White, a journalist, novelist and playwright who at that time was also Assistant Controller and who came to television from the *Irish Times*; and finally the recently appointed Programmes Controller, the Swedish Gunnar Rugheimer, who had come to RTE from the United States to take up the post at the invitation of the then Chairman, Éamon Andrews.

The interview took place in January 1964; the television service had been in operation for just three years. It was held in the conference room above the studios in the original television block in Donnybrook. It turned out to be a most pleasant and free-ranging discussion; rarely have I enjoyed an interview so much. I was asked all sorts of questions about my journalistic and creative work as well as about the ins and outs of governmental and administrative affairs — John Irvine, like myself, had been a civil servant and knew the administrative scene well.

At this remove, the only question of importance that I remember was one asked by Gunnar Rugheimer. 'So you've got this job,' he said, resting back in his chair, 'and you're in here with us. Tell us now what you're going to do with it!' I daresay the years of administration were no disadvantage in helping one to anticipate such questions; and to deal with them with the awareness of that anticipation. Half-way through my answer, he stopped me with a wave of his hand. 'You've said enough,' he told me. 'If you can achieve even half that, you'll suit us fine!' The course of the remainder of my working life was determined.

PART TWO

9
OUR MAN IN HAVANA

THE DECISION to leave the civil service and go to RTE was taken in a situation which I now see was compounded of some naïveté mixed with a very deep and real sense of idealism. The naïveté was probably more culpable: I had after all seen some of the tough grind of political life at reasonably close quarters in my civil service years. Having worked with men like Dr Jim Ryan and Seán MacEntee, I could not pretend to be wholly ignorant of the contorted and implacable nature of political life; in this respect, I even prided myself that whatever else would get to me, that would not. (I use the word 'political' in its wider sense, relating to the whole complex of management of human affairs.) But, despite such seemingly informed contact, I am bound to say that I remained largely innocent of its real complexity. Certainly, I was innocent of any knowledge of *television* politics, arguably the most complex of all!

This applies to more than Ireland. A favourite story at the BBC told how two former colleagues who had worked together in the regional studios in Scotland met again after many years in the corridors of the BBC's Television Centre in London. 'Have they stopped stabbing each other in the back up there yet?' asked the one who had been longest gone from the Scottish region. 'Good God, man,' was the reply, 'they stopped that years ago; they're stabbing each other in the face now!'

At the time this did not much worry me; in fact a short time before the result of the interview was announced, I had a call from Francis MacManus, then Features Editor in Radio Éireann, with whom I had built up a close relationship, based largely on the excellent letters of critical appraisal he wrote me about some of my earlier work. In one such letter he had complimented me on a story I had sent him saying that it was 'very Daniel Corkery-ish — and far too good for the rather casual

95

hearing it will get on radio!' I thought it might be about this story he wanted to talk to me when he rang and asked me to lunch.

The lunch turned out to be a bottle of red wine and a quarter pound of cheese; it was not the only thing about that meal that was unusual. For what MacManus wanted to tell me was that he had heard on the grapevine that I was about to be offered this job — and was I really wise in taking it? He could, when he wanted, be unusually candid: I recalled him later when I heard that BBC story from Scotland. 'That place out there is a snake-pit,' he said. 'And, as for the language, no-one in authority wants it. They'll pretend they do and pay lip-service and make all sorts of public statements, but in the end they'll do nothing. Your position is going to be impossible. One crowd will devour you if you don't do something, the other crowd will devour you if you do.' It was not a pleasant thought; yet so far from dissuading me, the idea of being caught between two such hotly opposed factions seemed to promise a lively and interesting time. That I should not be put off by it seemed to surprise him, so he went on to add weight to his dissuasion by pointing out the unique position I was now in. 'As I understand matters,' he told me, 'you're riding the two horses — and managing it well. You're an up-and-coming civil servant, and your writing is being accepted all over the place. That's a rare combination and one you should be slow to change. If you go out to that place,' he warned, 'I promise you you'll never write another word in your life!'

This was a most chilling prospect, but how could he be so sure? How rarely one heeds the advice of others when it comes in the form of something one does not want to hear oneself! After the years of apprenticeship, struggle and failure, and eventually some success, I did not think that the stream could now ever dry up. (As it happens, I was right: it is not conflict and contention that stops one writing, but apathy, indifference and the content-ment of too much ease.) So I told him I did not feel I had too much to fear in all that. There might even be an important difference of emphasis between me and some of the other can-didates, I said, when it came to dealing with such stresses. And what, he asked in evident surprise, might that be? 'Well,' I told him, 'others may think this job is about language or music or entertainment or literature or culture or something civilised like that. So far as I'm concerned, I believe what I'm entering is *politics* — okay, television politics, but politics just the same. And that's a trade about which I may just know the least little bit.'

On the afternoon of the very same day, I had a call from Riobard Mac Góráin of Gael-Linn. Bob was an old friend from my time in University College Cork. I had become reacquainted with him during his time as editor of the Irish-language magazine *Comhar*, for which I wrote theatre and film reviews. What he had to say to me was that his chief, Dónall Ó Móráin, wanted to talk to me urgently about some interesting news they had just heard. It didn't take much guessing what this was about; it lent weight to the view that I was to be in for a most interesting time!

Ó Móráin was a name of seminal importance in the whole developing language scene. Some people would say that he had brought it single-handed into the twentieth century; certainly Gael-Linn had created a series of highly successful entre-preneurial ventures in fish-farming, film-making, records and tapes, and the small but dynamic theatre in Stephen's Green — this aside from quite outstanding work in the field of direct language teaching — and all from a weekly lottery based on Gaelic games. His name was synonymous with what was pro-gressive and forward-looking in what most people saw as the hidebound and conservative language scene — so much so that people who had no time at all for Irish had a great deal of time for him. There was another point in his favour: a short time before this, with the assistance of Noel Mulcahy, a tele-communications engineer and friend of Tom Hardiman, who subsequently became Director-General of RTE, he had put in a bid for the new television service, a bid that proved a relevant factor in stymieing the foreign consortia that had tendered for this most lucrative concession — thus leading eventually to the establishment of the statutory RTE.

All this was in my mind when I went to meet him on that late spring afternoon in 1964. This, I felt, was not a man to be trifled with; he would not want to waste his time on niceties. There would have to be a practical, a positive spin-off for the language, which was his prime concern in everything he did. He was said to be ruthless; his ruthlessness, I had been told, included the removal of anyone who got in his way. Was I to be one of them? So far as I was concerned, there could be no doubting what that way was: it was that the Gael-Linn bid to influence television in the interests of the language and nation, which had failed, would be given a new lease of life by using me. Between us, provided I was willing to play, we would eventually succeed. It was, I could see, going to be a most entertaining talk!

Once again, it was to be most refreshingly frank: he wondered, as Frank MacManus had done, whether I would be at all wise in taking on this job. There seemed to be an awful lot of people about who, with my best interests professedly at heart, did not seem to want me to achieve them in quite this way! In Ó Móráin's case, he expressed surprise that one of the better-known applicants for the job had not got it — some of whom, I happened to know, were experienced broadcasters with a long history of language affiliation behind them, which I had not. From the language point of view, they might thus be thought to be more amenable to language-organisation thinking.

That was perhaps one reason why they had not been chosen. For one of the questions put to me at the interview touched upon this very matter. Gunnar Rugheimer, who, right then, was getting a hard time of it about the language from Authority member Ernest Blythe — who in turn was taking stick from the language movement for *his* inactivity — asked me quite pointedly if I were a member of any of the Irish-language organisations, which were being quite belligerent at the time; I could sense that my answer would prove crucial. As it happens, there was only one answer I could give and that was the truth: the only organisation to which I had consistently belonged since coming to live in Dublin some twenty years before was the Sandycove Forty-Foot Bathers' Association! My impartial broadcasting future was assured!

In that first contact with him, I found Ó Móráin a most intelligent and perceptive man; also, I am bound to say, I did not find him at all the draconion manipulator some people seemed to think him. It was a help, of course, that we were of one mind about the language and its place in the life of Ireland. There was no doubting his deep and lifelong commitment to the restoration ideal: it was broader than that and included the whole wide spectrum of national concerns; but the language, both then and since, was the aspect that most needed the dynamic of so able a man. Whatever was proposed for the language within RTE could, he said, only be helped by appropriate pressures from outside. Considering the back-ground, composition, personnel and financial strictures upon RTE, on my own I might not be able to achieve very much; aided and abetted by help from them, I might achieve a great deal indeed.

At that early time, my position was a bit like that of the Fianna chieftain, Fionn Mac Cumhaill, whose power derived from a willingness to take help from wherever he could find it! 'Ná diúltaigh aon chabhair a bhfaighir' was his favourite phrase. If, when I got into it, Dónal Ó Móráin or anyone else could help me achieve the sensible programme of language development I would propose, then I would gladly accept. I did not perceive any undue deviousness or disloyalty in this; I believe in open argument and the power of persuasion. If a point of view I do not hold carries sufficient conviction for me to come round to it, then I am enriched and deepened by that experience. In this sense, I may indeed be rather more open to conviction than others; but I was naïve enough at that time to think that others would join the argument with an equal candour.

Before ever getting to the point where I might be drafting pro-gramme policy, however, I first had to learn something about programmes. So I was delighted when, coming up towards the end of my first month in RTE — it was the end of April 1964 — Gunnar Rugheimer rang one morning from Geneva, where he was attending a European Broadcasting Union meeting, to say that he had arranged a training course for me at the BBC; and on the following Monday — it was May Day — I presented myself at the BBC Training School in Lime Grove, London, where my education in television programme-making began.

I had not known quite what to expect. My knowledge of television was confined to what I saw on the screen, yet my awareness of the creative process was real enough, and I had no lack of ability in expressing it. I felt at home in the company of creative people but had small tolerance for the phoneys, pretenders and self-seekers who, in that early time in the life of television, seemed to proliferate. Even then some of us knew what we wanted Irish television to do; we wanted it, in Parnell's phrase, to expand 'the boundaries of the nation', to enrich, deepen, enlighten and educate our people — and to do this in a way that would be delightful, attractive and a pleasure to watch. In a word, we wanted television to shape and make a rich and sophisticated new Irish national psyche: not to be, in Seán Lemass's maladroit phrase, 'an instrument of Government policy', but an instrument, like government itself, in bringing the people to the very height and pinnacle of their powers.

It would be some time yet before I got to putting all this down in programme and policy form; but it was all there on that May morning of 1964 when I went to the BBC for the first time. Hence, while in a technical sense a neophyte, I was, in a conceptual and programme-making sense, probably quite mature and well formed. And this, along with the fact that I was from another country and another culture, made me, I think and hope, a fairly welcome addition to the all-BBC trainee group in Lime Grove.

My early writing days with the BBC had given me the impression of an organisation with a wide and comprehensive sense of corporate excellence; in Owen Reed's training school, I could see why this was so. The slipshod, the indifferent and the shoddy were anathema, the attitude that 'it will do' utterly abhorrent. One was taught to seek the ultimate perfection of everything by the inbuilt personal admonition: 'I care, that's who cares.' Over and above the technical side, one learned about quality of mind and judgement, that bright and sturdy dedication to truth that has made the BBC foremost among the broadcasting services of the world. This emerged even in the casual talk. Having just left the narrow confines of the civil service, it was a delight to be in the company of highly creative people such as Stuart Hood (then Controller), a quiet reflective man of adamantine integrity; the brilliant and ebullient Huw Weldon who, as well as presenting the arts programme 'Monitor', was also Head of Talks, a laconic title that covered the whole range of documentary and current affairs; David Attenborough, then a senior producer but clearly a broadcaster of world stature; Alisdair Milne, who has since become Director-General but even then could hold his own in any intellectual company in the world; Don Baverstock, who has since gone to Yorkshire where, I am sure, he still carries about with him the apparatus of the luminous and agile mind; and the redoubtable Grace Wyndham Goldie, that tungsten old valkyrie who had raised and nurtured them all.

I don't know if the BBC produces people of that calibre now. Broadcasting — or is it just life? — the world over seems to have bottomed out at a level of comfortbale and well-established mediocrity! But at that time those people in the BBC would have shone out as people of outstanding quality anywhere. I remember some years later being at a reception in the Hotel Europe in Monte Carlo during the UNDA Film Festival. There at the time among the guests was Brigitte Bardot and her new husband, Roger Vadim; also there was Susan Hampshire, who had recently become the television rage because of her success as Fleur in 'The Forsythe Saga'. But the moment Huw Weldon and David Attenborough came through the door, there was no doubting who the 'big people' were.

Don Baverstock, also of that company, was the great favourite of Grace Wyndham Goldie, who had done him no harm at all in his bid to become BBC Controller at a stunningly early age. Alisdair, some time before that, had made a name for himself as the astute and inventive editor, with Ned Sherrin as producer, of the brilliant and satiric 'That Was the Week That Was'. He is Scottish, a fact he will not let me forget by his insistence on speaking Gaelic — a language he learned in his maturity — whenever we meet. He is a delightful man, brilliant in speech and brilliant in creative silence; his scholarship and distinguished personal background sit lightly upon his shoulders; he is modest to the point of being totally self-effacing; but, having seen him in action, especially in his Glasgow Controllership days, I am in no doubt that there is a tough core of integrity there at the heart to ensure that the BBC's cherished traditions of integrity and truth are in very safe hands.

One day, in the midst of this course, I found myself in conversation with Don Baverstock and a number of others on the question of organisational structures, when the system of editorial control came up. With my background in the civil service still close to me, I tended to think of this in terms of a fairly rigid hierarchy in which responsibility rested at the top and was delegated along clear lines from there down. The man at the top in the civil service — the Minister, who is charged with implementing Government policy — got what he wanted; the element of personal vagary did not arise. In television, this did not seem to be quite so. There, what seemed to me a dangerous pseudo-democratic sophistry came across things, which in effect said 'Tot homines quot sententiae' — there are as many views as there are people, and one view is as good as the next. This was, of course, the kind of principle that made the Tower of Babel. I did not like it. I believed, and still do, in the principle of orchestration: one conductor for a multi-piece orchestra. We know what would happen in an orchestra if each of the players began to play his own tune; or, what is worse, if groups of players decided to create pressure to play their own tunes: when the noise of their discordance would deafen out the others and frighten the unfortunate conductor into thinking *they* were the orchestra, each an independent group to themselves.

All this was in my mind when I was talking to Don Baverstock that day. In the BBC, he told me, things weren't quite like that — though there were of course similarities. One remark he made to me at that time was so colourful that it still sticks in my memory. 'The BBC', he said, 'is not a hierarchy in the usual sense; it's more like frog-spawn, or the Vatican: cut it at any point with a knife and it will coagulate behind the knife!'

This strange description was soon to have a very real significance in my life. It so happens that one of the reasons why I had been recruited to RTE was that such a knife had been applied shortly before I came, and I was to become part of what would coagulate behind it. The urgency of that coagulation was intimidating. For Rugheimer had undertaken to provide the Authority with a new series of 'Teach Yourself Irish' programmes, and I was the one who was going to provide them. The best advice he had been given before that was that this was impossible: we hadn't the necessary writing skills; linguistically acceptable performers were simply not there; probably there wouldn't even be an audience. What people wanted was programmes in Irish for those who had the language; for the rest, they should be written off.

This made small sense to me. Only a few short years before, I had become interested in the language myself, and knew from personal experience what that reawakening had done; I could not abide the notion that others whose lives could be equally enriched should be denied that opportunity. So, though I was no teacher, and certainly no teacher of language on television, I did have a good disciplined approach to writing; I had some journalistic skills; and given the imminent deadlines, I had no choice now but to set about using them.

'Labhair Gaeilge Linn' has probably been forgotten by most people now. But in its time it was a highly successful venture. I was convinced that, if the language was to mean anything to the normal person of our time, it would have to be presented in a way that would appeal to the new urban-oriented mind. Its success was principally attributable to three elements: the late Father Colmán Ó Huallacháin, who planned the linguistics; the scriptwriters, to whom I had given clear lines of instruction to create lively and attractive themes; and Eoin Ó Súilleabháin, who presented it with vigour and style. Style, in this context, is the important word. The programme was running a few months when a letter arrived from a viewer, which summed up Eoin's contribution. 'Dear Liam Ó Murchú,' it said (mine was the last screen credit, as Editor). 'I like your programme "Labhair Gaeilge Linn". The man teacher is a real man, not like some of the pansies ye do have. Not that I believe in the revival of Irish. I think ye're flogging a dead horse. But, by God, that fellow is flogging him with style!'

Style was indeed what 'Labhair Gaeilge Linn' communicated: that sense of a language that had a place in modern situations and which young people especially could identify with. One series was set in a bedsitter in Rathmines, with Sinéad Cusack in the lead role; the next time I saw her on screen she was playing opposite Peter Sellers in her first major film. Her sister Sorcha joined her in that same series; the next time I saw her she was playing Jane opposite Oliver Reed's Rochester in *Jane Eyre*. A wonderful designer named Hywel Morris, who, being Welsh and knowing the problems of popularising a minority language in a world-language situation, cared deeply for what I was trying to do with the language in Ireland, designed highly attractive sets in an idiom that was unmistakably modern. Having caught that idiom, I could not go back on it.

While 'Labhair Gaeilge Linn' was still running, Colmán Ó Huallacháin told me one day that a new set of Irish lessons was being prepared in the Department of Education, based on the language frequencies found in his computerised study, *Buntús Gaeilge*. The script eventually arrived — whatever else it was written for, it was not written for television. But that mercurial man Donough O'Malley, who was at the time Minister for Education, wanted action on the language; by action he meant spectacular action, and he wanted it now. So he announced that there would be a new series of teaching programmes, without consulting anyone — and it then became my business to make television out of it!

In this, once again, I was aided by a superb group of performers. It was the age of the mini-skirt; and viewers will remember with what seductive style those girls wore them: Ruth Buchanan, Aileen Geoghegan, Máire Ní Néill, Bernadette Ní Ghallachóir (who later went on to present Ireland's first Eurovision Song Contest). The drawings were done by Bill Bolger and made fun where there was none in a dry-as-dust pedagogic script. All this was aided and abetted by a highly attractive booklet, the money for which was supplied by Charles Haughey, then Minister for Finance. He rang me after my request had been turned down by the officials of the Department of Education. Clearly, they did not believe that the number I had asked for — 250,000 copies — could be sold. He quizzed me briefly about the figures, asked about the selling price, which I had pitched at a shilling (5p) to ensure a huge print run — and then told me to go ahead, the money would be there. The whole conversation took less than five minutes. Rarely have I seen such an example of administrative trust. I know that Father Colmán had spoken to him before I did — in those days we were like twins, one of us rarely in action without the other.

The trust was justified. The whole print run of a quarter of a million copies was sold before the first series began. The programme ran three seasons at peak time and held top ratings throughout. Part of the reason why it was in short segments of five minutes' duration each was that viewers are more lethargic than they are resentful; the maximum length of an ads break is about three and a half minutes; they will not switch over to another channel for anything short like that. So much for linguistic engineering — and so much for those remote and scholarly experts who know a great deal about academic matters but precious little about the simple, publicly acceptable things of life!

All this was in the realm of language teaching, and I wanted to do a great deal more. Refresher courses in Irish were all very fine, but they were not what I had come into television to do. Yet I had been given the task; it would not be done if I did not do it; its success was as much a response to that compulsion as it was due to anything of mine. But so much more needed to be done to give the language a real and respected place in people's lives. It did not have that then. Most people had little time for it, many said they hated it, largely because of unhappy associations in school. Even amongst those who favoured it, the whole surrounding life — business, commerce, religion, entertainment, sport — gave them no encouragement at all. Once they left the school gate behind, the language, so far as they were concerned, was dead; and that was the national audience the programmes were going to have to address.

It was perhaps my good fortune that it had not been all that long since I had been in much the same state myself; all or most of my friends and relations still were. What I wanted to do was to put programmes on air that would communicate in acceptable form that process of re-education that I myself had so recently undergone: the songs I had learned to love, the poetry and stories that shed light upon the people who went before us, the very sound of the language that was so beautiful, especially upon the children's lips; in a word, to lift up the nation's morale, its sense of pride and confidence in its own people, of which the distinctive Irish language was an essential part.

I wanted to motivate people towards that knowledge by teaching them about the places they lived in, the names of townlands and fields and rivers and villages, of cities and streets too — all of which were blood and bone of the Irish experience, and only the language held the key to their meaning. I wanted to teach them the meaning of their own names, first names and surnames, many of which were meaningless without the language — yet the vast majority seemed to have turned their back on it, were wholly ignorant of its place in their lives, like some generation of amnesiacs who had been stunned into forgetting who they were a long time ago and could not be woken up to it now. Waking them up would be my task. I knew them well enough — were they not my own people? — to know that when they were properly moved by it, they would indeed respond.

These sublime and ethereal thoughts would not, however, make television programmes, unless I and my production teams could turn them into them. That would mean presenting them through the people, machines, studios, cameras, microphones, editing rooms, budgets, designs and sets that are part and parcel of the complex labyrinth of television production. The most important element in that was people. The best ideas in the world are no use unless you can have people of like mind who can put programme shape and make upon them. Nowhere is T. S. Eliot's phrase more true: 'Between the conception and the act falls the shadow.' I have seen so many shadows fall since that first dawn that I wonder now that I can still write with such enthusiasm about it!

As I saw it, we would have to plan for four programme categories. There was the living Gaeltacht, where Irish was the language of the home; in addition to that, there were individuals and homes all over the country where Irish was a native or fully fluent second language. That was one programme category — a minority of the national audience admittedly, probably a quarter or so, but enough to form an integral and recognisable group. Then there were those — undoubtedly the average viewer, and hence the great majority — who had learnt some Irish at school but, due to lack of practice, had lost touch with it; for them, programmes wholly in Irish would be a switch-off; but that did not mean that they would not want to hear any Irish at all. This was where the bilingual programme came in, its emphasis on entertainment, laughter and fun. Thirdly, there was a whole range of enrichment programming, aimed at educating viewers about the place of the language in the nation's life. And fourthly, there would be a need for language teaching programmes aimed at different groups and age levels within the audience range. Add to this a regular input of Irish-language content in children's programmes, and a consistent language presence across the programme spectrum generally, especially in continuity, sport and general entertainment, and we had the makings of a very satisfactory language policy indeed.

All this was thought out and written down, and it did indeed form the basis of whatever programme plans RTE had for the language in the ensuing years. But I repeat the Eliot phrase: 'Between the conception and the act falls the shadow'! That shadow has been over RTE for many years now. For it was in the implementation of this policy that all sorts of personnel and logistical problems arose. For all sorts of different reasons, people in crucial places didn't speak Irish and, lacking real concern for the language, were not as keen as I was to help develop it; I was often reminded of Thoreau: 'To make men zealous is not within the competence of law.' Some who did understand and were in many ways well-known Irish-language people stayed well away from an area that was widely reputed to be contentious and ill-endowed; nobody wanted to be associated with a range of programmes which, the general run of producers felt, had small resources, small audiences, and small organisational support. (An exception to this in due course, when it came on, was 'Trom agus Éadrom', which has been sustained over the years by the support of some producers, most notably that quiet but single-minded man, Denis O'Grady, who has been with me on the programme now for many years.)

Then there were the 'Gaeilgeoirí' themselves, some of whom seemed to feel that I was as much in their employ as in that of RTE — a kind of honorary, unpaid, Graham-Greene-like 'Our Man in Havana' — who had nothing to do but put on *their* Irish-language programmes, and automatically the audiences would watch! It was difficult to get them to understand that they would not. Unless attractive and winning in themselves — and sometimes even when they were — the sad experience was that Irish-language programmes would not be watched, would in fact be switched off. Gunnar Rugheimer used to point out the grimmest statistic of all: even in the single-channel area where they had no alternative but to watch RTE, there would still be a massive drop in audience numbers when some programmes in Irish came on. The TAM ratings were held suspect because of that: but they were a reasonably reliable statistical count, doing no more in this case than indicating that people would prefer to have nothing at all to look at than to look at programmes they did not understand.

When Michael Garvey did a production of Mairéad Ní Ghráda's *An Triail*, I did a survey of the ten plays produced in that season, in the hope that it would be able to prove that there was an audience for such plays. They were mostly plays in a lighter vein, such as Lennox Robinson's *The Whiteheaded Boy*. The only two plays of real depth and dramatic quality in that season were the play in Irish and T. S. Eliot's *Murder in the Cathedral*. The audience figures for the other eight plays were good; Eliot was second-last and low; but the play in Irish beat even that to the bottom of the list! It was this inventory that led a dedicated Irish-language colleague to remark that the plain people of Ireland seemed to prefer the Barrabas of high culture to the Jesus of the Irish language when it came to making their television choice!

I make these points in order to show that putting Irish-language programmes in the schedule will not itself achieve much. Where the language is dense and concentrated, it may even do harm, reinforcing in the general public mind the instinctive conviction that the language is not, and never will be, for them. The argument is only part-commercial — though it is, of course, that too. But no-one in the popular medium of television — where, by the very nature of the trade, one hopes for majority acceptance — rejoices at the thought of majority rejection. That switch on the television set is a most democratic instrument. When, as happens, one sees abysmally low viewing figures for programmes that are transmitted at what are quite reasonable, even peak, hours, then the message is perfectly clear that they are not what the plain people of Ireland want.

In the bilingual category — I exclude 'Trom agus Éadrom' for now, which is a story in itself — 'Amuigh Faoin Spéir' with gramme, 'Féach', smelted together in the mid-sixties out of a hotchpotch of junked newsreel and a paltry patch in the tiny Studio 3, won a consistent and appreciative audience. The producer, Eoghan Harris, whom I had helped bring into television in the first place, brought fire and commitment to the programme; as, later on, did Seán Ó Mórdha, whom I had brought in too; but, over the years, the most consistent link with the programme was Proinsias Mac Aonghusa — a man who, like his father before him, has a deep and abiding love for the language and everything national-minded in Ireland.

In the bilingual category — I exclude 'Trom agus Éadrom' for now, which is a story in itself — 'Amuigh Faoin Spéir' with Éamon de Buitléir and Gerrit Van Gelderen gained wide and enthusiastic approval. The programme series we did with Seán Ó Riada's Ceoltóirí Chualann (now the Chieftains) and Father Pat Ahern's 'Siamsa' in Tralee were imaginative and exciting presentations of Irish music and dancing in visual terms; and, in a quite different vein but operating from the same native inspirational source, the programmes with the Belfast engineer, Albert Fry, and that mercurial Clareman, Tony MacMahon, were a great success.

My own favourite amongst the enrichment programmes was a series called 'Watch Your Language', in which we aimed to

108

explain to audiences how and why the language died as a vernacular in the last century; and, with examples such as Finland, Israel and other revival successes in mind, how that need not be the end of things. In association with that series, I got together a lovely sensitive series of filmed programmes, scripted by Diarmuid Ó Muirithe, under the title 'Voices from a Hidden People'. This might be said to be a television version of Daniel Corkery's masterly *The Hidden Ireland*. Areas rich in literary tradition were selected to show the direct link between the literature in Irish and the contemporary lives of the people. It was a moving series of programmes — the kind of thing I had most come into television to do. When, in the closing programme of that series, Diarmuid quoted the beautiful and passionate lines of the Spanish poet Lorca on the unique place of a native language in a people's life, it was a statement very close to my own heart.

Some time later, when I was asked to talk to a new RTE Authority about the place of Irish in the programme schedule, I concluded my talk with this clip as a superb example of what we should be about. Picture my surprise when one member found this exquisite and sensitive piece of work 'racist and fanatic'; and declared that he would be 'terrified' of placing responsibility for television programmes in the hands of the people who devised it!

Such then were the joys of having become Editor of Irish Language Programmes in RTE. The successes were few, and all of them hard-won; the abortions, miscarriages and outright failures many, and too bitter to bear remembering. Frequently throughout those years I was reminded of Yeats: 'How small a part of our culture can be brought to realisation and even that little but with a great pain, in a much-divided civilisation'! Television, I'm afraid, is a bit like that: only a little of what is hoped for and dreamed of ever comes to pass. It took me a long time to come to grips with this; in those early years I tended to feel a bit sorry for myself in that, first of all, I cared so much and, second, that I could only rarely get the support and practical encouragement that the beleaguered language required; at such times, I tended to feel that I was fighting a lost and losing battle, which did indeed cause me much distress, including one serious illness; but I am a healthy creature, not wholly without a sense of humour; and my personal and family life has always been a bulwark against such things. Also, I made some fast friends. I shall always remember with love and esteem that most elegant of men, Pádraic Ó Raghallaigh, who stood with me throughout — even though it was commonly thought I had been brought in by Rugheimer to replace him. John Irvine was a cool and constant friend who, in my view, should have been Director-General twice over but never was. Perhaps in his way, having been bred in a mould of proper order and control, he was somewhat at odds with the new galloping liberalism that the sixties and early seventies ushered in.

The permissive ethic had become rampant not alone in television but throughout the whole of society then and made it a most difficult time to institute order and control. I believe I am right in saying that Dr Tod Andrews once remarked that he had found RTE a most trying place to get the things he wanted done. Dónall Ó Móráin, when he eventually left the chairmanship, summarised his position on radio one day by saying that quite simply his 'writ did not run'. The notion of industrial democracy, pepped up under Michael O'Leary's term as Minister for Labour, for a time became a kind of galloping consumption wherein everyone's interpretation was as good as that of everyone else! One whimsical remark of that time was that participation had been brought to the point where almost the only people not allowed to participate were the ones on top! This, as can be seen, was most unfruitful ground in which to cultivate the largely unwanted language; and the foolishness or innocence of those of us who were committed to it in writing down policy that there was no real stomach to implement was indeed destructive of one's early enthusiasm and hopes.

In the midst of all this, what helped to keep the creative side of my own life alive was that I had already endured several earlier, far drier, years of civil servitude. Throughout those later times when — whether it was true or not — I felt I was something of a lone voice seeking a fair deal for Irish as well as firm editorial control within the television programmes division, I often thought of that remark of Don Baverstock, that television was 'like frog-spawn or the Vatican: cut it at any point with a knife and it will coagulate behind the knife.' I was in the middle of many such cuts, yet happily lived to tell the tale. I dare say it will be a longer tale before I am done! Maybe that is why, when I wrote earlier about 'the at once imperilled and protected person I am', I may be telling no less than the truth!

10

THE HUMOURS OF
DONNYBROOK

THE HISTORY of television, in Ireland as elsewhere, is a minor history, and its detail as nondescript as that of most other businesses. The glamorous world of the 'stars', once it gets into the minutiae, loses a great deal of its glamour, and the 'stars' turn out to be minor enough constellations — highly movable too — in the real world in which they live. I shall spare you the boredom of much of what I know of it except when it crosses up with this particular tale.

Already, Don Baverstock's colourful remark had suggested that the process would not be an orderly one; yet nothing quite prepared me for some of the disorder that characterised those early years. How much of this was due to the fact of its being a new service trying to find its feet, and how much to a basic uncertainty not alone within the broadcasting world but in the community at large about what the salient values of Irish broadcasting should be, are indeed moot questions. Certain it is we did not seem to have the same faith in our own creative people as the BBC had — a situation sometimes compounded by the people themselves, by a certain disjointedness and lack of ballast in their general make-up. Nevertheless, one repeatedly felt that the creative, the artistic, the instinct and talent for entertainment should all have been advantageous for high office; while technical, financial and other ancillary skills should have been seen as services to the central conceptual role. Too often it did not seem clear that that view of the proper priorities was held. It always seemed strange to me that, apart from the first, and most extraordinary, Director-General of the BBC, Lord Reith — who was indeed an engineer but, oh, so much else as well! — all the succeeding top people had worked through the creative and journalistic fields. This undoubtedly led to a pre-

111

eminence of the conceptual, and placed all the ancillary roles where they should be: as services to it. Hence the highest point of the BBC hierarchy was the ability to conceive broadcasting policy in programming terms and thereafter place in due order realistic plans to implement it; whereas in RTE, buildings, machinery, equipment and the financing of them seemed to play the more salient role. It was this reversed order of things that led Maev Conway to remark one day at the end of a long and tedious discussion on the expanding capital programme for new studios and equipment, with little or no time left to discuss what programmes might go into them, that RTE would end up 'a solid gold Cadillac — with no petrol to put in it!'

Kevin McCourt, perhaps more than most, did not want this to be so; he was in fact a most frank and engaging man. In his very first interview after he had been appointed, he told the interviewer he could 'blank him on that' when asked about his approach to programming and a philosophy of broadcasting; he did not know much about these things — management, the proper disposal of staff and resources, was his trade — and was honest enough to admit it. Nevertheless he had fine instincts, and would have responded well to a programme philosophy worthy of a national broadcasting service, had he been given one. On one occasion, the morning after we had put together a programme with Seán Ó Riada entitled 'Freedom and the Rights of Man', he rang me to say that that was the kind of nationally uplifting programme he had hoped for when he decided to take up Éamon Andrews and Seán Lemass's offer to come to RTE in the first place.

It was during those early years that the question that has foxed enquirers of all shades down through the years often occurred to me: who runs RTE? Not since Kevin McCourt's first Controller, Gunnar Rugheimer, has there been anyone who went at all near supplying a single answer to that highly complex question. Gunnar was direct, forthright; he was an insatiable worker, and he had an extraordinarily sensitive nose for the Irish political scene. In the space of a few seasons he had launched four new award-winning series: 'The Riordans', 'Telefís Feirme', 'Telefís Scoile', and my own series, 'Labhair Gaeilge Linn'.

I rather suspect that his consuming interest in developing the agricultural scene stemmed from the fact that Charles

Haughey — whom he admired and who at the time seemed to some to be on his way to becoming Taoiseach — was Minister for Agriculture and wanted to enlist the powerful instrument of television to create a whole new and enlightened approach to their business by the recalcitrant Irish farmers. In this — unlikely a Haughey ally as he may now seem! — he was ably abetted by Justin Keating, himself a veterinary surgeon and a man of compulsive communicative ability. Justin was willing to take on the task of educating the Irish farmer on his own! But as inventive people tend to do, Gunnar made many enemies on the way, which was a great pity because they might have just as easily been his friends. Eventually — it is all recorded in *Sit Down and Be Counted,* Lelia Doolan and Jack Dowling's book — a movement built up against him, spear-headed by some activist groups within the main producer unions. I remember well the day when things came to a head — unfortunately, I played a not insignificant role in it.

It was during a meeting to review progress on planning for the forthcoming autumn schedule. There were delays on filming plans due to the fact that there was no supervising film editor; interviews, we were told, had been held in London and, I think, a number of other English cities in order to attract one.

This seemed to me to be a rather unusual proceeding. Had we, I asked, no such thing as a potential supervising film editor of our own making at home? Or, if we hadn't one right then, should we not think of training someone to become one? Gunnar resented my intrusion; coming from someone who was thought to be his protégé — what was more, someone who was a comparative newcomer to the scene — what did I mean holding up his meeting like this? But it *was* as it happened something I felt rather strongly about. The service had been in existence for some years now; there were in my view, and in that of many others, far too many non-Irish people still about; surely here was an example of a comparatively straight speciality which we should be able to provide from among the film editors we ourselves had in RTE, or in the country generally. Gunnar was clearly displeased with this, and said so. 'I want you to stop this right now,' he said. 'This is not a matter for which you have any responsibility.' The trouble was that, as an Irishman in a new Irish television service, I saw myself as having a very clear responsibility — a responsibility that I knew was shared by many

113

of my Irish colleagues around the table. Perhaps, however inadvertently, there was something maladroit about the way I put it: 'We built a world airline here on the strength of Irishmen,' I said. 'We built a hydro-electric system, the first of its kind in the world, on the strength of Irishmen. Surely to God we can build a minor thing like a film editing system on the strength of Irishmen?'

Though I hadn't meant it that way, Gunnar saw a challenge to himself there; when the meeting was over, he asked me to come and see him in his room. What in effect I was saying when I spoke like that, he said, was that *he* was not the man for his job — was that what I really meant? It was not time for prevarication; in any case he himself was direct enough to deserve better than that. It was, I said, my belief that sooner or later an Irishman would have to be found to fill so vital a post; there was no point in beating about the bush about it. Would I, he asked, be willing to keep this view to myself over the coming months, when some crucial decisions would be made? I knew he was talking about his own contract, which was up for renewal just then. I said I would by all means be discreet but, if asked, could not think or say otherwise than I had done. Then suddenly his tone changed as, to my great surprise, he told me that, of all the people in RTE whose support he could not afford to lose, he could not afford to lose mine! I held, he said, the key to that vital language-nationalist constituency without whose approval in the current climate no Controller could hope to survive! It was heady stuff: I think he believed it; I certainly believed that he for his part was a good Controller — after all the years, I still believe the best and most inventive Controller RTE ever had; yet I also believed — and, despite all the traumas of the intervening years, still believe — that so vital a job in the national broadcasting service should be filled by someone who has a natural, not acquired, sense of the Irish people and their complex cultural past. He left a short time afterwards; there was a new Authority, and his friend Éamon Andrews was gone by then; and with their going, RTE entered a whole new and volatile phase.

If what characterised the régime of Kevin McCourt and Gunnar Rugheimer was a certain stern authority and a single dominant view, the period that followed was marked by a diffusion of responsibility that tended to make everyone something of his own master. This was not as alarming as it sounds: for one

114

thing, it was part of the temper of the time. The late sixties was the era of personal freedom, even when that freedom took on the most bizarre and idiosyncratic forms. Professor Tom Murphy, then President of UCD, tells how, during one student 'riot', he was on his way to a conferring when he actually got a boot in the backside from one of the joyous rioters; in any normal situation, whoever did it would have been expelled, but Tom, being the sensible man he is, knew that his backside would recover whereas the unfortunate expellee might not — so he wisely advised a less condign retribution.

Revolt was not quite so flagrant as that in RTE; but, perhaps in concert with the same concessive temper, Michael Garvey as Controller and Tom Hardiman as Director-General communicated the feeling that creativity flourished best in an atmosphere of maximum liberty — a good and positive belief but for the fact that it was a liberty that sometimes took little account of the age and life-experience of those on whom it was conferred. A new trainee brought in today was involved in running programmes of national importance a year from now; and people who had little more than the bloodless life of the university debating scene behind them were being entrusted with matters of real flesh and blood very early on. This was encouraged, was even thought to be educative; if mistakes were made, then the learning process happened all the quicker.

On one occasion — it was an introductory seminar — Tom Hardiman surprised us all by telling us that he was proposing to present two of his more fiery particles, Eoghan Harris and Colm Ó Briain, to Judge Murnaghan's Commission of Inquiry to give them a taste of the kind of creative powder-keg over which he had to preside. The result was explosive but extremely funny, the new bloods of the Commission eyeing with something less than favour the radical new bloods of RTE, and the radicals, knowing that they could not be touched (they had strong union support), taunting them with the promise of further defiance. In another situation — a theatre, perhaps, or a university — it would have gone down fine; but in a national broadcasting service, whose very objectivity had only recently been called in question by a judicial inquiry into a programme on moneylending, it made for a very choppy situation indeed. Eoghan Harris, in a black leather jacket, and pale with the

115

fervour of his latest crusade, declared that there was no such thing as an impartial documentary, it had to have a committed point of view; he left one in no doubt what his point of view would be. Colm Ó Briain, elegantly raffish in a canary shirt and with a bright cravat slung about his neck, went on to exemplify what *he* meant, by showing a clip of film in which, as I remember matters, he had championed the case of the Gore-Booth sisters in their claim against the Forestry Department against what seemed to me substantial legal facts. The Commission chairman, Judge Murnahan, sat there wordless — but, to those of us who knew him, growing steadily more apopleptic with what undoubtedly seemed to him such cavalier insouciance. He was not in a court of law now — a fact that clearly inhibited his style! If ever I saw an occasion when a judge would have been happy to pass summary sentence with condign punishment, this was it. John Irvine quietly scribbled on his writing pad — I often wished I could have read those notes!

Afterwards, I had coffee with a few members of the Commission, who informed me that, on the basis of that showing, they would have no hesitation in putting in a report on RTE that would be sufficiently scarifying to gut it for all time! What they did some years later — by which time Tom Hardiman, with great skill and charm, had sweet-reasoned them out of their rage — was to put in a report that guaranteed that when the second television service came, it would come to RTE and no-one else.

So much for the hot flushes of those parvenu custodians of the public weal who are sometimes set upon the backs of the long-suffering broadcasting fraternity to keep them in check; and so much for the dire predictions of those hurlers on the ditch when, in a moment of brief glory, they get in there to play the game themselves!

Since I mention some names, I should say that I myself was partly responsible for bringing some of these people into RTE in the first place. In that earlier, troubled conversation I had with him, I had said to Gunnar Rugheimer that, if his credibility as a Controller of Irish television was to be made secure, the first thing he must do was to get creative young Irish men and women into the service, preferably people with some sort of proven ability in the broadcasting trade. The first intake included Lelia Doolan, Dónall Farmer, Muiris Mac Conghail

116

and Deirdre Friel; the second, Eoghan Harris, Brian Mac Lochlainn, Seán Ó Mordha and Dick Hill. All of them went on to make fine programmes, some to advance in the administration, later on. Some got caught up for a time in the galloping revolt rampant in the sixties; and this, combined with a loose and sometimes over-indulgent management, produced disconcerting waves.

The Irish proverb 'Is minic a bhain duine slat a bhuail é féin' — a man often cut a stick to beat himself — sometimes proved uncomfortably true; a process of hierarchical leap-frogging built up in which people began to distrust each other, and where people of like mind were set, almost deliberately it sometimes seemed, at each other's throats. This did not help organisational unity. That, more than anything else, is what a national broadcasting organisation needs. Neither did it help the process of programme gestation, which requires a good deal of inter-personal trust. On more than one occasion, I put forward programme series which, because of this, turned out to be quite other than I intended. One was a series of interviews with notable Irishwomen. The purpose was to create in the public mind the image of dedicated women who, while successful, educated, and outward-looking, would also be national-minded in the best and most sophisticated sense; the women I had in mind were people like Siobhán McKenna, Neillí Mulcahy, Justice Máire Roche, and Máire Mhac an tSaoi. The idea was taken, then handed over to someone else to produce, when what emerged made me so sorry I had initiated the idea that I swore I would never do it again. Another series about place-names and their meaning, which would light up whole areas of Irish life, was put out in a way that became a skit and a mockery on the educational and meaningful thing I had in mind. I did not lose sight of my ideals in the middle of all this, but I certainly learnt how to move more carefully!

Those were the years when I began to regret the loss of Gunnar Rugheimer: he had a deep conviction about broadcasting and the primacy of the essential broadcasting function, that is, the conceptual, in the hierarchical scale. Michael Garvey was nothing if not creative: he has in fact an extraordinary polymath mind which is as much at home with the most recondite arts as with the most complex technologies; but it would not be doing him an injustice to say that management

117

and administration were not exactly his first love. In any case, he had never wanted to be Controller in the first place. He was a brilliant producer whose special strength was in drama; shortly before his appointment he had done a stunning production on small resources of *An Triail*, a very headline of what television drama should be all about. But I am afraid that in those years he became caught up, like the rest of us, in the new 'democratic' principle of everyone's voice being equal to everyone else's — which tended to make our programme councils into something like a high-class Tower of Babel! A single convinced informing mind in control would have been able to say what he wanted Irish broadcasting to do and, with that central conviction, be able to assign priorities of people, money and facilities to do it. Instead, what there was was a plentiful supply of resources — those were the years of surplus finance — a strong but necessarily inexpert layman goodwill on the part of the Authority, and a hundred disparate and conflicting ways of using it.

I tried to get more effectively into this scene by applying for a number of jobs that would be central to it, notably that of Controller when Michael Garvey left; predictably, however, this was filled by his assistant, Jack White. On one occasion, thinking that it might at least give access to important overall policy thinking, I applied for the newly created job of secretary to the Authority. In a brief monosyllabic interview with Dr Tod Andrews, he held me with steel-blue eyes and a face gnarled from age and old fighting, while I told him of some of the things that I thought would have to be done before RTE could be got right. Maybe it was too much for him. Maybe there were indeed less painful ways of bringing about the desired results. (In effect my ideas were more or less what the Stokes, Kennedy, Crowley consultants recommended when they reported on the organisation many years later.) Anyway, he rejected me. He said I had far too much creative drive to be wasting my time in administration when I would be better placed in front-line programme-making. All he wanted, he said, was someone to sit at meetings and record the notes; even as he spoke I knew perfectly well — and I believe as old and seasoned a campaigner as Dr Andrews knew — that there would be a great deal more to it than that; but it was a fair enough position for a Chairman to take at the time, though strangely at odds with events as they

118

turned out. He appointed Oliver Maloney — like myself an ex-civil servant, with a further short spell in another semi-state body; Tod was said to be brilliant at divining unknown talents like that.

Oliver did the job for a number of years, and difficult years they were, with all the usual tensions between the executive, in the person of the stylish and courteous McCourt, and the Authority, in the person of the tough, intellectual and straight-talking Andrews. It must have been some crucible to come through — but come through he did, and went on, after a spell as Head of Personnel, to become the youngest, and in some ways the best, Director-General RTE had. This was but eight short years after he had come to us as that unknown and anonymous official, who would keep the Authority's notes, whom Dr Andrews said he had in mind when he spoke to me.

The process of change continued, quickened in fact as the years went by. Oliver moved with firmness and decision when some of the powers that had made him turned on him and had to have their wings clipped. He had a slow, drawling way of speech which belied a quick and able mind, but, again, his predicament became increasingly difficult as he was caught up in the new 'democratic' principle that every man's word was as good as the next.

Tod's successor as Chairman was my old friend Dónall Ó Móráin. An Authority policy document on Irish was drawn up — looking at it, and the modest nature of its demands, one might whimsically reflect upon that phrase of Ovid's about 'the mountains being in labour to produce a ridiculous mouse'! But whether mouse or mountain, it came to little in the event as the pressure of more urgent organisational matters such as the increasingly complex industrial relations scene and, of course, the vital lifeline of finance, pushed it out to the peripheries of everyone's concern. Meanwhile, a new Authority, appointed by Conor Cruise O'Brien, was in office, and Dónall found himself surrounded by colleagues who, he subsequently publicly stated, deeply distrusted him and believed that his main purpose was the limited language aim; in turn, in the course of that radio interview of his, Dónall stated that he was caught up in the *realpolitik* of a structure where the power was not effectively in his hands, where he was necessarily held at arm's length by senior staff, to say nothing of other colleagues on the Authority.

119

All of which was of course complicated during the tenure of Conor Cruise O'Brien as Minister — a man whose attitudes then to the language would require the talents of a Myles na Gopaleen or that more ancient paragon of scalding misantrophy, Bricriú, to describe. On one occasion — it was a Jacob's Awards function in Waterford — he drew the whole language establishment down on him with his infamous 'monolithic bog-oak' speech, a speech at one and the same time so pithy and so maladroit as to set both friends and enemies at his throat! He seemed to see the language as a creeping growth, laden with injustice and cruel imposition upon an ignorant and long-suffering people. And, at a time when the rest of us were hard put to it to hear a word of Irish in public anywhere, he seemed to find the whole of Ireland tentacled by its strangulating claws, with the unfortunate English tongue in imminent danger of extinction by its further advance in the cloying world of television!

The Authority has of course the overall responsibility in all this, and that is set out in the governing statutes. By now this is supported by a solid and well-formed code of custom and practice. Their relationship with the staff and the programme-making function is a book in itself, but it may be no harm to say just a few things here. There have been superb Authority members, people of genuine quality of mind who had that breadth of vision and integrity that ensures high-minded and impeccable judgment. Theodore Moody was, I believe, such a man; so was John Robb and, though more laconic, the legendary Dr Tod Andrews. It would be too much to expect that all members would be of that quality: they are, after all, meant to be custodians of the public trust, and should not be expected to be much bigger or better than the public they serve.

One does hear the criticism from time to time that some of the people appointed have no experience of communications, that they have never produced, written or edited a word nor had any connection with the production trade at all; yet they become all-important governors of broadcasting overnight. It can indeed be disconcerting for the broadcasting fraternity — a docile enough herd — to be swung into new and uncharted waters according as new powers begin to emerge, with an interest in, say, the semi-states or trade unionism or the halls of entertainment or whatever — to say nothing of the even more strident voices who want to sing the unholy psalms of straight profit-and-loss! It is difficult, as can be imagined, to keep a constant course in the midst of all this. But, by and large, Authority members are people of good judgement and experience, appointed by the Government of the day to do a difficult and time-consuming job; they do this for a pittance — is it still £800 a year? — and precious small thanks. It is not a job anybody in their senses should want.

I have heard some of them described from time to time as 'political hacks' — but, even if they were that, there is absolutely nothing wrong with it provided they are also people of good judgement and an overall sense of national responsibility. True, as with the jury system, there can be exceptions: people with a preponderance of interest in particular concerns that push other concerns to the outer margins. The programme critique in such cases can sometimes deteriorate into a too-particular, often splenetic, resentment of things with which they do not personally agree. But direct intervention from the Authority in programme matters is rare. I am not entirely certain that this is always right; there have been times when one would have welcomed some more direct indication of Authority interest in the main matter in hand — that is, the programmes themselves. And, for what it is worth, my own advice to Authority members would always be that, if it ever came to a choice between reading the back-breaking mounds of documents that necessarily form a lot of an Authority's work, and looking at or listening to individual programmes on air — then choose the latter! That is the real and only bedrock upon which a proper critical assessment can be based.

Undoubtedly, the canvas is too large, one can touch it only in spots. Sheila Conroy came along after Dónall Ó Móráin, following a putsch in which the unfortunate Dónall was ousted; the overt reason given for this at the time was that he was keeping too much to himself and not letting the Authority in on anything; for his part, Dónall stated that the executive was keeping too much to itself and not letting him in on anything! So it went on, round and round the mulberry bush like that in a recurring change of fortunes. My own fortunes changed as well as the rest but whatever chance I may have had with earlier régimes, there seemed little or none for me once the anti-Ó Móráin group got going in the early seventies.

That, effectively, seemed to be the end of my career prospects in RTE — but for the marvellous, warm-hearted Sheila Conroy. Sheila became, first a member, then Chairman, of the RTE Authority. She was a Bantry woman, working-class to begin with, but from her trade union experience — she was ITGWU president John Conroy's wife — she was shrewd, level-headed and with an astute political mind. During her time, I became Chairman of Comhairle Raidió na Gaeltachta, subsequently Assistant Controller under Jack White, but more than all of that, by her consistent advocacy of the bilingual approach as the only sensible way to advance the language with mainstream audiences, she was the one who really made my television programme, 'Trom agus Éadrom'. Thereafter, her support, encouragement, her tough and plain-spoken advocacy of what I was trying to do to bring the language out of the ghettos and into ordinary people's lives gave me the sense that at long last there was someone at the top who knew what the 'plain people' were about and would take no notice either of cliques or begrudgers in helping one reach them.

But all that is a separate story, which in some respects goes on to this day. Hence it must have a chapter to itself.

11
OUT IN FRONT

' AN RUD IS measa le duine, b'fhéidir gurab é lár a leasa é'; the Irish proverb puts it well. Or if you prefer Saint Paul: 'The things that are to thy peace are now hidden from thine eyes.' The Section 31 directive, Kevin O'Kelly, and IRA Chief of Staff Seán Mac Stiofáin, were all to have a strange and far-reaching effect upon my life. For it was these events that were to trigger off another restructuring within RTE, the long-term result of which was to launch me upon a new and exciting career.

Long before coming to RTE, I had of course been writing, and in those early years had done a lot of work for Radio Éireann and the BBC: but the job I took on in coming to RTE was a purely administrative one and, apart from some occasional creative and journalistic work, I did not see myself becoming involved 'front-of-house' at all. Then, at a time when the Government were pressurising the media, expecially RTE, not to give coverage to the Provisional IRA, Kevin O'Kelly — one of the most responsible and trusted journalists in RTE — interviewed Chief of Staff Seán Mac Stiofáin, his clear intention being to aggressively question the purpose and effects of their shooting and bombing campaign; whereat the Government became so incensed that they sacked the whole Authority and introduced the now notorious directive under Section 31. This in turn was followed by a whole new internal restructuring within RTE wherein control of all current affairs programmes was removed from Controller of Programmes Michael Garvey and placed under Jim McGuinness, Head of News, and his Deputy, Desmond Fisher; in the process I lost 'Féach', whose development I had fostered over many years. I was cross about this: I felt I had helped steer the programme from small beginnings to where it now was, an important programme of current affairs; I had helped contain its talented but mercurial team and, though frequently in trouble because of their radical and iconoclastic bent, had never once let the ball into the net. Now the programme was gone and there was nothing I could do but accept it.

The withdrawal symptoms were painful and went on for quite some time, until Michael Garvey suggested one day that the best way I could come out of it was by taking on a programme myself. The idea of a programme administrator presenting a programme was unusual, but Michael thought I could manage it. There would probably be the usual objections to it by vested interests within the service: the word 'demarcation' was darkly mentioned; but, all things considered, he felt I could handle it.

In effect, I had recorded my first show in Studio 3 before anyone knew I was doing it at all! It was a straight face-to-face talk-show called 'Gairm' — meaning 'vocation' or 'calling' — in which I interviewed people in Irish about the shape and make of their lives. It went fine for a time, then gradually it began to burst at the seams. One can of course make a show with a few people talking, but it's mostly a bore unless you can make them do something else as well. That could be a song, music, dancing, painting: laughter is probably the best of all — anything that enlivens the atmosphere, the more entertaining the better. And if this is true for ordinary programmes, how much more is it true with Irish-language programmes where one has to work to hold an audience all the time!

So, for example, Gearóid Ó Tuathaigh of Galway is a historian and a scholar: that much is or may be known about him; what is not known is that he is also a fine step-dancer. Éamon de Buitléir is a wild-life film-maker: that much is known about him; what may not be known is that he is a fine musician, especially with the slow Irish airs on the mouth-organ. Putting those pieces together made a much more entertaining show; audience response showed that this was right. Gradually, the idea gathered momentum. Soon it was clear that the tiny Studio 3 was not able to handle all that was going on. So Jack White, who had become Controller by then, encouraged by the always supportive Sheila Conroy, came to me one day and asked if I could expand it by increasing the number of people, and perhaps even having an audience in. That was how 'Trom agus Éadrom' began.

It moved then to the rather larger Studio 2 with, in the very first programme, the late Seán Óg Ó Tuama and his friends; this was a marked improvement, from my point of view. It was the usual format for a television chat-show: some entertaining or meaningful talk, some music and other entertainment, the whole welded together around a single person or theme.

That autumn, the programme moved to the more spacious Studio 1, and subsequently went on outside broadcast locations around the country, where it was most popular with rural audiences. When given the advantage of a good transmission time, it was a TAM-topper; it won a Jacobs Award (presented by my old colleague, by then Minister for Industry and Commerce, Justin Keating). The eve-of-All-Ireland programmes were hugely popular, as were such programmes as the one on the 1914–18 war, the one with the missionary societies around the world, and many of the outside broadcast programmes (for which I have to thank Joe Barry, Head of Outside Broadcasts, and his dedicated crews).

Over and above all else, the bilingual aspect of the programme is still thought to have been a milestone in the progress of the language. This bilingual approach originated when viewers began to sense that the programme was one they could enjoy, and began to ask increasingly if I could sub-title it or at least give them some inkling of what was going on. I knew from my own experience that most people's school Irish was rusty from lack of use, but that did not mean that they did not want to hear the language and occasionally even attempt, when the opportunity offered, to speak it. How, if not in this way, was the public for Irish ever to be increased? And how, if not by this means, was the desired national aim of restoration ever to be advanced?

My own experience had taught me that fluency is gained only with practice, and practice can happen only if the good speakers are willing to help the bad. That was how I had become fluent myself: should I not try to do the same for others? Should I not try to create the climate in which people would become aware of what 'the hidden Ireland' could mean to them, its language and poetry, its music and songs — things that had come to mean so much to me? Maybe I was excessive in this hope. Maybe I placed reliance on perceptions which many people do not have. I do not think so. There are literally thousands of letters, some deeply moving letters, telling me that 'Trom agus Éadrom' gave people new inklings of what the language might hold, and new motivations towards helping develop its growth.

The position of the vast majority of Irish people today is that they know enough of the language to make a beginning, but how can they progress from there unless they are given the opportunity to try? The bilingual approach is the one sure way this can happen — a fact that was enthusiastically endorsed by the broad general audiences the programme won. One had to be careful not to press them too far, otherwise quite simply they would switch off; the willingness was there but the fluency was not. One had to start from some sort of bilingual base. They could progress from there when given access to reasonable opportunity to try. But how could they even begin to try except in the company of those who already do speak the language and hence have the capacity to pass it on? How long is the myth going to persist in some quarters that you either speak Irish perfectly or you do not speak it at all? In learning language, as in learning anything else, you creep before you walk — a set of stumbles and starts that are aimed at eventual fluency, which is achieved in this way and in this way alone.

It was the success of 'Trom agus Éadrom' that mainly led the then Minister for the Gaeltacht, Denis Gallagher, to ask me to take on the chairmanship of Bord na Gaeilge in the autumn of 1979. I had no wish for this office, being far too busy with my radio and television work (I was also running the daily 'Slán Abhaile' on radio at that time). But I did see the need for a dynamic and innovative Irish language agency: something that would motivate ordinary people to renew their interest in Irish and re-create in our time the spirit of the founding fathers of the Gaelic League. In fact some years before — back in the early sixties, when we were on holidays together in Ballyferriter — I had given Professor Seán Ó Tuama, at his request, a paper that he was passing on to George Colley, then Minister for Education and thought to be close to De Valera in Government thinking on the whole language issue, in which I proposed a dynamic new Irish language development board that would have a core of entrepreneurial executives, much on the lines of the then infant IDA; this board, with the assistance of the voluntary movement, would push the language forward into a new bilingual era. This, in effect, is what Bord na Gaeilge eventually became; but, by now, I was far too busy with my own radio and television work to

126

readily accede to the Minister's request; decent man that he is, I put him to the lengths of his having to ask me three times before I said yes.

The reason I eventually did so was essentially the same as had brought me to television in the first place: I wanted to help make the language a reality in the lives of ordinary people all over Ireland. I saw the predicament of the teachers in the schools and the parents at home endeavouring through the educational system to teach the language in a way that would make it possible for the children to pass examinations and eventually get jobs, then finding no use or purpose for it once the school gate was left behind. This seemed to me an appalling waste: a waste of time and resources in teaching, a waste of cultural enrichment because the teaching did not work. At least *I* could see this later point, could see the language and its worth as an instrument of real cultural enrichment; the vast majority of people did not. Hence, we had a whole nation involved in an exercise that seemed of little or no value to them — and this at a time when the valuable hours spent on it could well be spent learning something else, a foreign language perhaps, which at least would have some commercial or tourist value later on.

I saw Bord na Gaeilge as a powerful new instrument for changing all that; I saw it heralding a new phase of language development, in which Irish would begin to appear in the shops and business places, in industry, commerce and tourism, in farming and trade union life, in local government, health and social welfare, in banking and finance as well as in churches, places of sport, recreation and entertainment — in a word, everywhere that people worked and lived the ordinary, everyday life. That was my intention and it consistently remained my intention throughout.

It was an intention that was clearly favoured, and I made some fast friends. Frank O'Rourke of the Bank of Ireland was a concerned and sincere helper, with a discreet eye for what would help the language in the influential banking scene; Vivian Murray of the Irish Goods Council, Tim Mahony of Toyota, Feargal Quinn of Superquinn, Paddy Galvin of Guinness — all gave valuable support. (Who does not remember the marvellous Guinness ad, 'Tá Sé Ag Teacht'; Tim Mahony's 'Veain an Tí' and 'An Ball Atá Mall sa Toyota', or the greetings in Irish at the checkpoints in all Feargal Quinn's superstores?) Gerry Jones of the Jones Group was a concerned and active helper; he it was, with Vivian Murray, who brought all these business people together in the first place — including Michael Smurfit who, in one whirlwind day, gave us an inkling of how *he* could make things shift when he wanted to!

In the area of local government, county managers Dick Haslam of Limerick, Noel Dillon of Wexford, Frank Molony of Donegal, Michael Boyce of Carlow, Séamus Keating of Galway, and Paddy Donnelly of Kilkenny were all steady and effective supporters; while Jim O'Mahony, secretary of the Department of Agriculture, and Tom Coffey of the Department of Finance — now governor of the Central Bank — also gave important support.

None of these people would have had any previous connection with the language, any more than I had; but the minute I approached them, they were more than willing to become involved. Yet such is the abiding perversity of Irish life that this fact seemed to be resented by some of the more rigid establishment-minded Gaeilgeoirí; they seemed to feel that the language was the preserve of an élitist few, and the closer it was kept the better it would be. I paid small heed to this constricting view and carried on with what I was trying to do. I felt I was on a right course and, given time and support, could hope to see it lead on to what I had for years now been seeking: a genuine expansion and development of the language amongst ordinary people throughout the whole of Ireland. So far as 'Trom agus Éadrom' was concerned, the programme had proved the rightness of my approach, and by now had won such national esteem that any guest I asked was delighted to come on.

When the programme went on outside broadcast down the country, literally thousands flocked to it; no matter how large the halls we played in they were always packed. I recall wonderful nights in Drumshanbo, Dunmanway, Limerick, Ennis, Monaghan, Galway, Thurles, Cork — everywhere the crowds came and clearly enjoyed the singing and dancing, as well as the readily understood bilingual chat. I became widely known as 'Bualadh Bos', and would hear it in the most unlikely places. Once, a row was about to break out between rival gangs at a match in Cork, when suddenly one of the lads spotted me and shouted: 'Stop it, lads, Bualadh Bos is watching'! There and then a *bualadh bos* was set up, which instantly defused the impending conflict!

I encouraged both panel and audience to use what Irish they had, and it always worked. This undoubtedly led to some bad Irish being spoken — but that was the very thing I wanted: for how could bad Irish become good Irish unless it was tried out? The eve-of-All-Ireland programmes were especially vibrant — it was impossible to cater for the huge crowds who wanted to come. My favourite guests were the unsung heroes, the men and women who were doing something in their own community and not getting much in the way of recognition for it.

But we had the celebrities too: Jack Lynch, both as Taoiseach and Leader of the Opposition, came on several occasions; it was for me always a personal pleasure to have him. He knew our family well, especially my eldest brother, Kennedy, of whom he still speaks with warmth and affection. He knew the Uncle Jimmy too during his coal-yard days, and kept up the connection during his regular visits to Páirc Uí Chaoimh where Jimmy still turned out in his Saint John Ambulance uniform, though well into his eighties, for all the big matches. Charles Haughey, too, was always a welcome guest. I still recall a wonderful night with Ruth Ó Riada, Seán's widow, and Seán de hÓra of Ballyferriter; we went on afterwards to Club Chonradh na Gaeilge in Harcourt Street for a great night of Kerry singing and dancing. Garret FitzGerald was a most engaging and pleasant guest — I have always been fascinated by the story of his extraordinarily national-minded parents, both of whom, from widely differing backgrounds, were in the GPO in 1916. Also most welcome was Cardinal Ó Fiaich, an old and dear friend who, in the phrase of Saint John of the Cross — 'contemplata tradere' — was always willing to share with us the fruits of his wide-ranging and scholarly mind.

All these varied streams were then running in my life. It was an absorbing and hugely busy time, but they were all things I had set my heart on — and I never therefore felt disheartened or tired. The family was growing, they were moving out of school and into university, some were already married; I might be forgiven for thinking that I had done my bit, for one lifetime! But for some time I had seen what I felt was a serious gap in the national life, one which, if given the opportunity, I would gladly have gone in and helped to fill. Politics, it seemed to me, was thin enough in people who cared deeply about the language and the whole cultural ethos surrounding the language to which I had now given half my life; lacking that drive at the top, it was inevitable, I feared, that it would lack it all the way down. If the opportunity ever arose to get into the front line there, the pattern of my life over the preceding score of years told me I would not turn it down. That opportunity was to arise sooner than I thought.

12

THE MOST HONOURABLE PROFESSION?

'PATRIOTISM,' Johnson wrote, 'is the last refuge of a scoundrel.' John F. Kennedy in another definition referred to politics as 'the most honourable profession'. It was probably because I saw things Kennedy's way rather than Johnson's that I decided to become involved. Before I had done with it, I began to see that there might be little merit in both!

The night Garret FitzGerald's first Coalition fell, in January 1981, I was in White's Hotel in Wexford, auditioning for a forthcoming 'Trom agus Éadrom'. I came up the stairs from the room where we had been meeting, and Michael Murray, who was my Wexford contact, told me that a general election had been declared. 'This is the one for you,' he said, and I laughed, never thinking he might be right.

I stood for Fianna Fáil, not because of any family associations — quite the contrary in fact. For old family reasons, I had of course a special affection for Jack Lynch, and in more recent years, during my time in the Department of Health, his brother Finbarr and I had been close friends; but then affection for Jack Lynch crossed all political divides. The connection with the Lynches in my life went back much farther than that. A small story about my mother best illustrates this. She had known and loved all the Lynch boys when they were growing up in 'Bob and Joan' under Shandon in Cork, and she was thrilled when my brother, Kennedy, who was Jack and Finbarr's age and had been in school with them, came home one evening and told her he was going up for election. 'Why wouldn't he,' she said, 'the decent boy! I knew the seed and breed of him!' But Ken then went on to say that he was standing for Fianna Fáil and the execrated De Valera. 'Not at all,' she denied. 'That decent boy never had anything to do with them!' Ken insisted, but to no avail. And to her dying day she went out and voted number one Jack Lynch, believing, as did thousands of other people like her, that no matter who he stood for, Jack Lynch could do no wrong.

My standing for Fianna Fáil, however, had very little to do with that. Quite simply, I had come to believe over the years that, overall, they had the more authentic national vision. I felt this especially with regard to the language, which had by now become central to my life. I wanted more imaginative and more committed efforts made towards developing it: towards developing the whole cultural national ethic, in fact. Fianna Fáil had of course their self-seekers, sycophants and lavish payers of lip-service, the same as the others; but in the end I did finally feel that there was a core of commitment there which I could further strengthen and tap. I had become friendly with several of the leading figures in the party, from my civil service days with my old boss, Seán MacEntee, to more recent associations with George Colley, Séamus Brennan, Michael O'Kennedy and, of course, Charles Haughey, who was leader now. As a civil servant I had known Haughey as a young Parliamentary Secretary working on the Intoxicating Liquor Bill. Later on, when he was Minster for Finance, I had developed a close rapport with him on matters associated with the language. I liked his direct and easy style, his warmth with people and his marvellous power of decision. He was, I felt, a man I could work with. (For what it is worth, Seán Ó Riada and, even more strongly, Father Colmán Ó Huallacháin with whom I worked closely on all those language-teaching programmes on RTE, had long ago formed this opinion of him too.) With Haughey in control, I felt I could have a real and positive input into the whole of governmental language and cultural thinking. That, so far as I was concerned, would be a sufficiently 'honourable profession' to keep me going for the rest of my life. So, when the request to stand came, I did not have much difficulty in saying yes.

The best thing to be said about the ensuing campaign was that it was the shortest in modern times, lasting as it did just seventeen days. That meant a whirlwind of activity, but it also meant one hadn't quite lost touch with the normal run of things when it was over and returned to base. Also, it happened in the first weeks of spring when the weather was not too severe. I remember only one day and night of torrential rain during which I was indeed soaked to the skin; but though friends remarked that in the radio interview I did at the concluding count, the cold I developed made me sound as if I were in the death-throes, I knew myself well enough to know that it was nothing more than the usual one everyone picks up, weather or no weather, at least once every winter.

The mental stress was another matter. I left Dublin on a Monday morning to be introduced to my fellow-candidates and begin canvassing that very night. By the time my wife arrived from Dublin two days later to be with me throughout the campaign, I already knew that this was not likely to be a life for me; but, having opted now for it, I would go on. It was not just the naked hostility of some so-called supporters — I had after all been imposed on them from Dublin — it was the hypocrisy, pretence and mock camaraderie of the whole sorry charade, of the constant need to ingratiate oneself in order to gain votes.

People asked for things they either could have by right, in which case the thing to do was to tell them their rights and how they should go about getting them, or else tell them they did not have a right and it was a deception to pretend that I or anyone else could somehow get around this and get them for them. In this I dare say I was too open and direct for the job; my life up to that had been the very antithesis of this. Both in the civil service and in television I had been my own man, serving masters by all means but keeping my own counsel and speaking my mind when I had to without fear of recrimination or loss; now I found myself in a very different situation, one in which there was little to admire, and nothing to be gained by responding to situations over which I knew I could have neither influence nor control. Being an extrovert by nature and for the most part a friendly person who enjoys company, I never tired of going from door to door and hearing people's troubles at first hand; that part of it I loved and believe I was very much at home with; but the mad rush and haste of it all made me feel a bit like those unfortunate priests in the confessionals on Christmas Eve in the old days, with the queues a mile long waiting to be got through and the slide going to and fro like a yo-yo as the poor men struggled to get through them all!

All this was of course necessary, from time immemorial it had been so; but this was my first brush with it and I didn't like what I saw. Not that I didn't have sympathy with the people

133

themselves: in many ways it was the very same atmosphere in which I myself had grown up; so much so that at every second door I was hearing things that were familiar to me from childhood. Also, with my old experience of health and social welfare, I was probably in a fairly good position to be able to advise; but, alas, there was little time for that: you had to rush on, shake hands with everyone who had a vote or could influence one, as if that were anything more than an empty ritual and of doubtful electoral value at that. Politicians have to do these things to be seen and get known, but there is surely nothing of substance in it, let alone that sense of national purpose that had got me into it in the first place. I was discovering this now — why couldn't I have done so before? Unquestionably, the idea of public service was uppermost, the sense of wanting to serve the nation in a way that would make it a better and more wholesome place for people of this and future times. There is a certain madness at the heart of this, but it is a madness touched also with a certain nobility. John F. Kennedy's 'Ask not what your country can do for you, ask rather what you can do for your country' makes the point well.

Coming to politics from television, I reminded myself that the same had happened with other ex-colleagues in RTE: Justin Keating, David Thornley, Ted Nealon had in their time been well-known television names. Knowing the performing arts can be no disadvantage when it comes to the public side of a politician's life. What was more important from my point of view was that I also knew the administrative side. Not many TDs walking into the Dáil for the first time would have the experience of having worked there before and of knowing the whole legislative and parliamentary process. I had done the spadework for several Ministers and knew the civil service thoroughly at first hand. I would never be making that classic maiden speech of the newly elected — knowing only too well how few were listening! I would have known without being told that the point of consequence for a new TD was in committee: an intelligent one who did his homework there could indeed make an impression. There were no headlines in it — and far too many public representatives are hung up on that — but it came to the notice of important people, and gradually built up a reputation. I particularly remember Senator Jim Dooge as being excellent in committee, his amendments always thoughtful and well considered. Seán MacEntee surprised me one day by saying that we were getting to the point 'where everything put down by Senator Dooge is proving acceptable'; that from MacEntee, no lover of Fine Gael, was some accolade!

So to say the least I would enter the scene not a total greenhorn, and certainly not one of those 'food converters with no other function but walking in and out of the Tá and Níl lobbies', as one of our number would flippantly describe deputies whenever he heard the division bell ring! (He didn't have the traumas they had in getting in!) But whether as one or the other, I would do so in the constituency of Cork North-Central where, though it was the place where I grew up, there would be very black marks against me. The blackest undoubtedly was that I had been imposed by Charles Haughey, not perhaps Jack Lynch's favourite man; for the constituency of Cork North-Central would be the fief and dukedom of Jack Lynch for all generations to come.

This in fact was where the whole story began. For no sooner had rumour of Jack Lynch's impending retirement started than the air became alive with talk of successors. The first tentative feeler I had about this came after a hurling final in Cork when a man I did not know, but subsequently learned was director of elections in the constituency, came up to me and asked if I would be interested in standing. My response was non-commital: interested, yes, but not to the point where I would want to push my interest against serious objections; if it was going to happen, then it was going to happen without my having played too active a role. That way, the element of fate, providence, whatever you like to call it, would be shaping things, and I myself wouldn't have pushed too hard or too far. That has pretty well ever and always been my view, responding to the nods and pressures of life, but once set upon a course going with it all the way; in this sense, one co-operates with a clearly defined force. If that is true Christian philosophy, so much the better, because I have always lived my life according to it.

From then on my name began to be increasingly mentioned. This was a teasing enough experience, which certainly concentrates the mind. Did I really want to be involved? What would it do to my life? Clearly I would have to stop broadcasting: there was a rule about that. I would miss television; but that would be made up for by being actively involved in *real* public affairs. What was more important was what would happen to my personal life. I had lived very close to the family, the children as they grew up became good friends with whom we shared all our thoughts and living; now I would have to spend most of my time away from them. If they were to be with me at all, it would have to be in the rough and tumble of political life. I preferred not to think about it; there are always a hundred and one reasons why one should not do something, and none at all why one should! 'Cowards die a thousand deaths' — there are whole lives of unexplored richness in the 'good sense' of the cautious; given my previous history, I knew I would not refuse the challenge when it came. If I did, then I would spend the rest of my life looking back. All things considered, if a clear call came, there was only one answer I could give, and that was 'yes'.

A clear call did come. I was asked to come to a pre-convention dinner in Cork on Friday night; the convention to select candidates would be the following day. I had been sent for because some people wanted me and saw in the well-known face the chance of a good poll; but some did not, because I was seen as a carpet-bagger, an interloper from the slick world of television, with no time at all for people in the real world like them.

It is extraordinary how people can polarise things to their own way of thinking. Those who wanted me went about in fear of being seen by those who did not; contact with me had to be in dark and furtive whispers, usually around corners or behind closed doors. I spent one whole session locked in a huddle in a hotel kitchen, with the honest chef and his staff wondering to God what programme I had on to bring me into their kitchen on top of them! When the huddle was over, people slipped away quietly in ones and twos: whoever was seen with me would thereafter be a marked man. Conversations were terminated in mid-sentence when the malevolent eye of an adversary fell upon my intruder scene. I was of course conscious of all this but, being an independent-minded person, did not take much notice: I could go on in the knowledge that public acceptance would be all that would count in the end, if and when I got out on the public scene. But this was where I made my first and most serious mistake: for the party would control the public scene too.

Party solidarity would, I was convinced, ensure support for the whole team; this seemed to me no more than good electoral common sense. But good electoral common sense in such situations, I was to learn, was not always the norm. And in any case, as was to emerge subsequently when Des O'Malley's Progressive Democrats party was founded, the Fianna Fáil of that time — and in Cork especially — was deeply divided within itself. And I, being the nominee of its leader, Charles Haughey, was in the very front line of assault for that whole deep-seated division. Hence it was that, when Liam Burke, a family friend but also a Fine Gael TD and so my adversary, met me on the canvass one night and told me I needn't worry about them, they would take nothing from me they had not already got, I began to wonder what he might mean, until suddenly he added: 'But for God's sake watch out for your own crowd, they're the ones who'll do you!' I laughed at the time, never thinking that he might be telling me no more than the plain truth!

For that first night, however, sufficient common sense prevailed to see the advantage of the well-known name. So a caucus was formed to draft me, a proposer and a seconder were found, one or two old friends got in beside me with words of genuine encouragement, which gave a fleeting promise that all might yet be well. For a time, when the issue seemed still in doubt and they couldn't seem to make up their minds who they wanted — and in particular whether or not they wanted me — a local headman got up and flung his hat on the table and swore he would settle their hash for the whole bang lot of them by getting on the phone to Jack Lynch there and then and ordering *him* back into harness! Now would they get off their asses! He got as far as the phone, but wiser counsels prevailed.

After that, things settled down a bit. We repaired to a pub in Blackpool, though it was well up to closing time, and there an even more passionate argument broke out on the relative merits of the 'Glen' and the 'Barrs' for the honours of that year's county hurling final. People kept on floating in and out of the discussion — even the venue moved. The next thing, we were all in a Chinese restaurant next door where, as well as ourselves and a totally independent hurling caucus, the local gardaí were also being fêted. For once, there was no doubting who the main attraction was. The proprietor, with mandarin courtesy, ceremoniously introduced me to all and sundry, and made a speech in which he said what an honour it was to have 'Mr Trom agus Éadrom' himself in his house; very soon, he predicted, he would have the further honour of saying 'Bualadh Bos' to his very own TD! I hoped the kingmakers were listening! His sons stood beside him, clean as ancient warriors, and as I left bowed to me as if I were some sort of latter-day Chinese emperor! I don't mind saying I was quite genuinely moved. It was the one fragment of instinctive welcome I had had in a difficult time. Maybe it was small comfort, but I felt that of one thing I could be sure: in the constituency of Cork North-Central, my childhood home, whatever the rest of the electors there might do, the Chinese vote was all mine!

I did not win the nomination; but by now this did not surprise me. Before it ever began, one man, who refused to give me his name, crept furtively up beside me as I sat alone in a dark corner of the hotel where the convention was being held. 'You take the advice of a fool, what you never took,' he said, 'and get out of here fast while there's still time. These people don't want you, it's as simple as that. So far as they're concerned, you're a Charlie Haughey get — they'd cut your throat if they had their way! They'll do that at the doors anyway, even if you do get on the ticket. So just get up and go while there's still time!'

Should I have done so? He was right — there *was* still time. I could have pleaded that, at the last minute, I had had second thoughts, and in all the circumstances felt it better to pull out. Fools rush in where angels fear to tread, one voice said; another, fortune favours the bold. Which was right? I am rather with Hemingway: 'A man does what he can'; perhaps I would add, 'and what he must'. In all this there is a providence, and one thing providence abhors is a lily-liver; nothing good can ever come from that, nothing but boredom, refusal, inanity, a slack and defeated sense of what life is or should be about. Like my father before me, I am a fighter; that means that one may indeed win or lose; but one thing I will not easily do, and that is give in.

Meanwhile, the fun and games of the convention continued. Like the old movies, there is, I am told, always a 'big man' at such events. At this one, he moved about warm as a slug, in and out of the whispering caucuses, and only once deigned to address me; this was in words of such stunning clarity that I there and then set them down and committed them to memory for the benefit of future postulants. 'Why don't you eff off out of here,' he said, 'and not be making an effin' eejit of yourself and everyone else? If you want to know, we'd far rather see the seat go to the opposition than see it go to an outsider like you!' He hadn't rightly finished when a soft-spoken lady came up to me and hinted that there might yet be ways into his heart — an organ she assured me he had. Would I care to make a subscription? The bigger the scrip, the nearer the heart: did I take her point? I was, I could see, getting closer. But I still had a long way to go.

Another anonymous well-wisher stepped up to me in the bar and said he commanded a block of a dozen votes; they were all mandated, he told me, to go in there and vote against me. Politely I enquired why this might be so — and he replied, also in words of sterling clarity: 'What effin' use will you be to me when I'm in trouble, and you away off in your big job above in Dublin?' There was clearly no point in telling him that being of use to him was not what a TD should primarily be about; so instead I enquired, still politely, what kind of trouble he might be in? 'Well,' he replied, 'right now I'm on a drunk-driving charge — could you get me off that?' I asked what his alcohol level was. He thought this pure evasion but I insisted, and when eventually I prised it out of him it turned out to be near incendiary. 'If ever I get to be a TD,' I said, 'the first thing I'll do is ring up the Minister for Justice and make sure fellows like you are locked up.' I could, I felt, say it with impunity: even with the Father, Son and Holy Ghost on my side, that block of votes was well and truly gone!

Anyway, the convention was held, and I lost. Those who know conventions will know what happens there. The process is that a party chief, usually a Minister or Shadow Minister — in this case it was, surprise of surprises in Jack Lynch's constituency, Des O'Malley! — takes the chair; nominations are put forward and voted upon; tellers go off to read the entrails and report the news. The chosen one is then applauded, while the rejects, suitably praised, promise party fealty forever. It all happens in an atmosphere of high excitement and great secrecy. Rarely in any coming together of people have I seen such whispering behind hands. As a television person running a big audience show, I shake hands a lot; but television has nothing on this. There is a great need for ingratiation: it is no place for introverts. Even if I was one before, television would have knocked the introvert out of me; but whether or no, in this game clearly I was not the stuff political stars are made of!

In those dreadful convention hours, I thought much about

Shakespeare's Corialanus, confronted with his craven plebs and their opportunist shifty tribunes. Not that I look at all like Corialanus — for one thing I'm too small; for another, I couldn't fight my way out of a paper bag. Come to think of it though, some of my antagonists filled the bill as those tribunes well enough: one of them, a thick-set fellow with the face of a bull-terrier, was given to quick spurts of speech owing much to the lingo of cowboys. In a brief access of confidence to one of his group, I heard him threaten to 'round up a posse and run this effer out of town!' Who knows, maybe this is how true tribunes speak? It was not, I was to discover, some idle threat: that posse subsequently turned up and descended on us one night out on the canvass; it consisted of several equally simian friends and relations, all well attuned to the same cowboy lingo; the gentle sentiment of 'running the effer out of town' was vehemently repeated; one marvelled at the richness and diversity of their language. What qualifications and training, I wondered, were needed to equip one to become a public representative in a situation like this? A prize-fighter perhaps? Or one of those all-in wrestlers who can take tackles front and rear and not be too upset when flung clean out of the ring? I began to have visions of myself slung up at the end of a rope or lying at the bottom of a quiet trout-pool on the banks of my own lovely Lee. It was clear that Coriolanus, television chat-shows, and even the quite reasonable knowledge I had of the whole governmental and parliamentary scene, were poor training for the distinguished role I was now about to assume.

To make a long story finally short, the convention voted, and I was rejected. So I could go back to my own life now, knowing, in the only certain way one can ever know such things, that this was not a life for me. That night, back at home, I felt a load lifted from my shoulders. I had given my fate the necessary chance, and my fate had said no. It was, however, in Robert Frost's words, 'a road I must go down'. I had gone down the road and been turned back. So, I could return to my own life now — that was the end of the affair.

Alas, it was not. By Monday — the convention had been held on Saturday — the whole scene had dramatically changed. Séamus Brennan, ex-secretary of Fianna Fáil and as experienced a practitioner as they come, had once said to me that if ever I wanted to become involved, I should not have to go before a convention at all. By its very nature, the convention depends on blocks of pre-mandated votes, which the local candidates have already secured. Someone nationally known such as I was would not need to go at it this way; once the party knew I was interested, I would be imposed in a suitable constituency when the time came. Jack Lynch had done this as Taoiseach; Liam Cosgrave, Garret FitzGerald, Brendan Corish, had all done it in their time; if I were interested, Charles Haughey would certainly do it in my case when the time came.

Eventually, that was how things turned out. The director of elections in Cork North-Central rang me on Monday to say my name had been added; a few minutes later, Albert Reynolds, national director of elections, rang to confirm that this was so. I can see now in hindsight what all of them must have seen all along — that I would indeed get a certain personal vote; that in all probability it would revert to the party if I were eliminated, so at least the established deputies would be secure. There was a chance, if I did well, that they might even gain a seat: that would be all to the good; but I doubt if, in the raw political game, anybody was thinking much about me at all.

So I went on the canvass and shook hands and was welcomed everywhere. Charles Haughey came on a whistle-stop tour and showed his characteristic loyalty by choosing to sit beside me at the lunch-table where we instantly became involved in deep but, as it happens, fairly innocuous conversation; by so doing he appeared to single me out as the favoured son. Later that evening at a press conference, when asked why he had imposed an 'outsider' against the local wishes, he replied with the same characteristic loyalty that I was an experienced administrator with many years of civil service work behind me; besides, that I had made a contribution to the cultural life of Ireland, the language especially, which was nationally recognised. With each word of praise, I could hear the long knives being sharpened. There would indeed be a night for using them later on! But, meanwhile, there was no doubting the pull of the television face; at one stage, a reporter following the canvass around predicted that, if it converted to votes, I would easily head the poll. This understandably did not appeal much to my fellow-candidates who stood to lose their seats if it were true; thereafter — I gather it is the custom — raiding parties went in wherever I had been to convince people that whoever else they voted for they needn't vote for me, I was already there. This, upon occasion, had a touch of genuine pathos; in one house, I was pulled inside the door where an old man said to me: 'There's five number ones for you here, boy — and that's for them that's gone. But don't tell the crowd outside that — they're all around the place here trying to blacken you!'

Those must have been some of the 2,000 votes I got — not all that bad, I am told, for a first outing, though not nearly enough to reckon in the final count. I rather think the reason I did not do better was the more obvious one: that the other candidates, living in the constituency and having worked it for years, *deserved* support far more. It was a heavy social welfare constituency where the problems were health and housing, unemployment and social benefits; whoever had delivered small favours on these things was going to get support. Quite simply, I had not. It impressed me in the case of one of the candidates especially (who subsequently became lord mayor) how frequently people thanked him for the good turns he had done them when we went to the doors. One could well see how they were indebted to such a man and would return it in the only they could: by helping him with their votes at the polls. And I am bound to say that the amount of work such men and their families put in in looking after these small interests was genuinely mountainous, and well deserved the backing it earned when it came to election time.

So I stood, and was not elected; and all the high hopes I had for getting to the centre of power and helping to change things must now go for nothing. Inevitably, I fell to asking myself later on what would my advice be to others like me — and there are lots of them — thinking of political life; and inevitably, alas, my advice would be that they should not. They will be hurt in the process, their careers will suffer, they will have nothing for it in the end but the experience of much hardship for their consider-able pains. The exception is where they have already grown up with the scene and are inured to some at least of its more injur-ious side. In this regard, I believe the uncompromising rigours of top-rank hurling greatly helped Jack Lynch; I believe his Dublin football years, his innate and indestructible personal toughness, as well, indeed, as the experience of watching his father-in-law, Seán Lemass, at close quarters, greatly helped Charles Haughey; Garret FitzGerald came from a household that was born of political strife — in any case, some will say he was propelled into politics by the most consuming factor of all — a compulsive talent for persuasive talk!

But, for the general run, none of this holds true. And since they can't all get in, it is important that they have other ways and other accesses to help as best they can to advance the public weal. For, meanwhile, there is a life out there to be lived and, if they are lucky, a great deal more to be done. It isn't only in the world of politics one can serve a country: people like the late President Cearbhall Ó Dálaigh; Sir Robin Day in Britain; and novelist Norman Mailer in the United States were all failed political candidates in their time. Promptly they all returned to the lives from which they came and went on to make an even greater impact there. Luckily, I had a trade to go back to, one I liked too. In the years that followed, once things eventually settled down, the fact that I had stood for political office only marginally affected my life. The great majority of people are fair-minded about things like that and appeared to have known why I had stood in the first place; and why, when I returned to television, I could honourably promote the same ideals and the same sense of national commitment that had led me to stand. For all that, it was with a certain sense of grief that I drove away from my own place on that last day of the electoral count, having been rejected by my own people. I hope that sounds as dramatic as it should: I certainly mean it to be. It was thirty-five years since I had first left home, yet in some ways I had grown steadily closer. I thought back to the days of my godfather Taidhgín spurring his horses on the rutted hill at Goulnaspurra, of the sweet singing of the choirs of my youth, of the men brawling in the lanes and the women with creels of fruit loaded like camels on their backs — they were all there in my mind as I drove up the road out of my own place on that last morning of my election defeat.

I had never hidden on television or anywhere else the fact that I was a Corkman; in fact in some ways I had been embarrassingly explicit about it. The language had, if anything, brought me even closer still — Cork names like Art Ó Laoghaire of Macroom (immortalised by his wife, Eibhlín Dubh's, Lament); O'Donovan Rossa and Michael Collins from Roscarbery; Terence MacSwiney and Tomás MacCurtain, who had been to the North Monastery, my own Christian Brothers school — they had all become part and parcel of the reawakened

143

and strongly national-minded person I had become. So far as I know, I was the first of my own people to reach back through the generations of the garrulous and disfranchised poor of the small alleys and back-lanes — like those true-born Cockneys born within the sound of Bow Bells, all my grandparents and their people before them had been from within a stone's throw of Shandon, the constituency centre: people who had endured through death and famine into new and terrible times, with their ancestral memory all but wiped out. These were my own people, blood of my blood, bone of my bone; I loved them and wanted to help build a new Ireland for and with them; and now I had gone down to look for their support and they had turned me down. All right, I hadn't given them time, had not prepared the ground while others by hard work and dedication had; that was true, all that and more; yet, what was equally true, and could now never again be otherwise than true, was that I had proposed myself to them and their decisive voice had said no.

It would, I knew, take time to adjust to the new situation. For one thing, I was no longer chairman of Bord na Gaeilge, an office which, as with all semi-states, automatically ceases when one is nominated to either house of the Oireachtas. What was more troublesome was that I could not now appear on television for a considerable time to come. There was a rule about that and, while it was applied, I thought, with particular rigidity in my case and for far too long, I could not deny that in principle the idea was right. I lost my eve-of-All-Ireland programmes, and regret the loss to this day; they were fine programmes, full of celebration and delight, and I must briefly put modesty aside and say in all sincerity that in my view those weekends are the poorer without them. But the weekly 'Trom agus Éadrom' started up again the following autumn, and was just as good as it had always been, especially when we went on outside broadcast. What was undoubtedly a fact was that I could put out of my mind for all time now the idea of further advancement in the hierarchy of RTE. I myself would have been the first to recognise that senior editorial office in the sensitive national broadcasting service required that one be seen to be outside and above politics. As it happens, I would have had no difficulty in separating my personal alignment from my editorial life: the old civil servant in me, if nothing else, would have taught me that. But, for the public at large, one must be seen to be independent, as well as in fact being so; and with the record of my political stand now behind me, I could see that that might not be so wholly obvious.

Here I was then, a shade over fifty, at the height of my powers; and, in seventeen short days, the whole world was a shambles about me. My sculptor friend, the late Séamus Murphy, used to have a phrase about Kinsale before that lovely town came back into its own away back in the sixties: 'Don't talk to me about that town,' he'd say in his inimitable Cork accent, 'Kinsale's future, like its past, is behind it!' Was I 'Kinsale' now?

In those dark days following the election, I shall not forget the loyalty of my own family, Cork and Dublin, and my dear good friends: Joe Barry, Finbarr Hill, Seán Ó Loinsigh, and the rest. On the night of my defeat we drank and sang our way into the small hours, celebrating just as we did after the great Munster finals — insuppressible always, in defeat no less than in victory. I have often thought that a great deal of the Cork psyche is locked to the same hurling, a game at which our players excel, but in the nature of things where we lose as often as we win. For defeat, far more than victory, teaches courage, resilience and equanimity of spirit.

I owe a special word of thanks too to *Irish Press* editor Tim Pat Coogan, whom I fortunately met in Jim Delaney's Dalkey Island Hotel the very morning of my return. Tim Pat had heard me on the radio the previous day — half the country thought I was dying when they heard that croaking choking voice! So, he proposed there and then to me an instant cure: like myself, he is a swimmer, and believes in swimming as the cure for all ills. 'Nobody is going to want you in RTE for a while now,' he said. 'So you can be free to meet me in the pool in Killiney Castle midday tomorrow and the same time every day for the next week. That'll drive colds and elections clean out of your head!' He was as good as his word: we met every day that week in Killiney and by Saturday the cold was gone. The day after was a day of brilliant sunshine and, even though it was still only February, there was a little heat in the sun; so I went swimming in the open sea in my beloved Forty-Foot — not the first time that blessed place had salved my drooping spirits!

That evening, with the new blood tingling in my veins, I began to write again; already, the sap was up.